PUBLIC SPEAKING

Public Speaking Tips & Tricks to Overcome Your Social Anxiety and Become an Enthusiastic Leader!

(Learn the Art of Effective Communication)

Andrii Penn

Published by Rob Miles

© **Andrii Penn**

All Rights Reserved

*Speaking: Public Speaking Tips & Tricks to Overcome
Your Social Anxiety and Become an Enthusiastic Leader!
(Learn the Art of Effective Communication)*

ISBN 978-1-989990-09-4

All rights reserved. No part of this guide may be reproduced in any form without permission in writing from the publisher except in the case of brief quotations embodied in critical articles or reviews.

Legal & Disclaimer

The information contained in this book is not designed to replace or take the place of any form of medicine or professional medical advice. The information in this book has been provided for educational and entertainment purposes only.

The information contained in this book has been compiled from sources deemed reliable, and it is accurate to the best of the Author's knowledge; however, the Author cannot guarantee its accuracy and validity and cannot be held liable for any errors or omissions. Changes are periodically made to this book. You must consult your doctor or get professional medical advice before using any of the suggested remedies, techniques, or information in this book.

Upon using the information contained in this book, you agree to hold harmless the Author from and against any damages, costs, and expenses, including any legal fees potentially resulting from the application of any of the information provided by this guide. This disclaimer applies to any damages or injury caused by the use and application, whether directly or indirectly, of any advice or information presented, whether for breach of contract, tort, negligence, personal injury, criminal intent, or under any other cause of action.

You agree to accept all risks of using the information presented inside this book. You need to consult a professional medical practitioner in order to ensure you are both able and healthy enough to participate in this program.

Table of Contents

INTRODUCTION 1

CHAPTER 1: UNDERSTANDING PUBLIC SPEAKING ANXIETY 2

CHAPTER 2: TRY GETTING RID OF FILLERS 13

CHAPTER 3: THE COMMUNICATION CYCLE IN TED TALKS 17

CHAPTER 4: HOW OTHER SPEAKERS, PAST AND PRESENT, CAN HELP YOU 24

CHAPTER 5: AUDIENCE 32

CHAPTER 6: THE AUDIENCE IS ALMOST ALWAYS YOUR FRIEND 43

CHAPTER 7: TREATMENTS FOR FEAR OF PUBLIC SPEAKING 50

CHAPTER 8: MORE TOOLS FOR SUCCESSFUL TALKS 55

CHAPTER 9: VITAL EQUIPMENT FOR THE PUBLIC SPEAKER 62

CHAPTER 10: SOMETIMES YOU WILL STINK 67

CHAPTER 11: THE PEOPLE AND THE PLACE. 73

CHAPTER 12: BODY LANGUAGE 82

CHAPTER 14: LISTENING AND STORYTELLING 87

CHAPTER 15: WHY BE A GOOD PUBLIC SPEAKER? 94

CHAPTER 16: THE LAYOUT OF THIS BOOK – ANSWERING YOUR QUESTIONS 100

CHAPTER 17: TECHNIQUES 108

CHAPTER 18: AFFIRMATIONS 120

CHAPTER 19: FAMILIARIZE YOURSELF............................ 128

CHAPTER 20: PRACTISING YOUR SPEECH – USEFUL TECHNIQUES AND EQUIPMENT. 135

CHAPTER 21: IT'S ALL ABOUT YOUR AUDIENCE 141

CHAPTER 22: USE OF VISUAL AIDS IN YOUR SPEECH OR PRESENTATION 148

CHAPTER 23: BOMBSHELL 152

CHAPTER 24: DON'T WALK LIKE A TIGER ON THE STAGE 157

CHAPTER 25: PRACTICE MAKES PERFECT 167

CHAPTER 26: PITCH PERFECT 173

CONCLUSION... 187

Introduction

If you have ever experienced stage fright and want a way to overcome that tense feeling. Well, I will teach you with a number of techniques that will not only help you prepare mentally but also actually help you start enjoying speaking in front of a large group of people.

Chapter 1: Understanding Public Speaking Anxiety

Different people call it by different names but they usually just refer to the same thing. Some of the terms that people use to refer to it include public speaking anxiety, speakers' anxiety, and presentation anxiety. Well, call it what you will but remember that you'll be dealing with the same symptoms and the same fear and excitement that can grip anyone who needs to address a group of people.

A Very Common Experience

Presentation anxiety is really a very common experience for everyone. It doesn't matter which part of the world you come from; you will feel some sort of excitement as well as a good degree of apprehension when you have to perform in front of people. Take note that feeling a little nervous is a very human reaction to a stimulus. Give yourself a congratulatory pat in the back; you're still human.

Being a little nervous can also be beneficial to the speaker. It keeps the speaker's mind sharp and on point so to speak. It will keep the presenter from being sloppy with his delivery and style. So, being anxious about your talk does have its own mix of the good and the bad. The important thing here at this point is to learn how to harness it as a positive factor and not let your nerves run you over like a stampede of wild bulls.

Here's a quick tip: All that nervousness will seem to immediately dissipate as soon as you begin to deliver the first few lines of your talk.

It usually happens to students but in reality it can happen to anyone. It can happen to actors, singers, athletes, politicians, scholars, soldiers, news reporters, police officers, and just about anyone you know. If you think that the fear of performing poorly in front of people is the province of private individuals who are not trained in speaking or otherwise presenting in public.

Even expert and seasoned speakers and notable talk show hosts that you see on TV get nervous from time to time. But everyone usually encounters this type of fear for the very first time in school. The class teacher usually asks students to things in front of the class.

They may ask a child to recite a poem in front of the class. Sometimes the teacher may ask students to bring something in front of the class and explain or talk about it (like a discussing a drawing or picture of their favorite pet). They may even be asked to something simple like reading a story. Everyone has to face it one time or another. However, the other option is to avoid this thing they fear throughout their lives.

Consequences of Avoiding the Issue

Avoiding a speaking engagement is definitely a terrible idea. It stunts one's personal growth. A lot of educators have pointed out to the fact that students who opt to avoid facing such anxieties tend to avoid it as well later in life. They usually avoid coursework and other study modules that will require them to speak in public.

When they attend seminars at school they usually don't participate in discussions. When they graduate, they tend to avoid jobs that will require them to do presentations. In fact, even when they are presented with a promotion to a position that will require them to present and speak to a team or staff, they will politely decline such an opportunity.

Remember that not dealing with this issue now will prevent further personal growth and maturity later in life.

The Symptoms of Public Speaking Anxiety

The physical symptoms of presentation or public speaking anxiety are very easy to spot. You can tell that you're experiencing this type of anxiety by its physical symptoms. Its symptoms include butterflies in one's stomach, visible shaking either of the body or hands (or sometimes both), getting tongue-tied dizziness, sweating, drying of the mouth, blushing, racing heart beats, and rapid breathing.

Of course the symptoms are not limited to these physiological conditions, signs, and symptoms. There is also a mental side to the issue that people can observe in them. When someone begins to experience this type of anxiety, one of their very first mental reactions is for their minds to go blank. It doesn't matter how many times you have practiced your speech and committed it to memory. We may even feel a little muddled as the anxiety builds up.

Notice that these are the very same reactions you can get when your body pumps out too much adrenalin. This means that coming up with a solution or at least a way to manage presentation anxiety will require a two-pronged approach. You will have to deal with both the physical and mental aspects of this condition.

The Center of the Fear

The next question that people would like to know is what it is that they are generally afraid of. When you ask people who suffer from this type of anxiety, they will tell you a variety of things but you will be able to point out a major common thread – the fear of scrutiny by their peers.

Some of these people may say that they are naturally shy. Others will say that they are uncomfortable being the center of everyone's attention. Some will say that they feel embarrassed for some reason. Others will describe their feelings as being self-conscious.

Some will say that they think that whatever it is they have to say is something that will not perk the interest of the crowd. Some people will even fuss about not being able to give what they perceive as the "perfect" speech (if ever there is such a thing. Some of these people will describe it as feeling that they will look "ugly" in front of an audience or at least that they will ultimately look stupid in the eyes of the crowd.

All of these reactions, if you try to look closer, only show that these people are afraid of getting unfavorable judgment. It represents our basic need of being accepted by a group and our general fear rejection.

Revisiting Abraham Maslow's Hierarchy of Human Needs

Abraham Maslow was an innovative psychologist in his day. He was one of the first experts in the field of psychology to shift the focus of their studies on healthy people. Previous studies in the said field centered mainly on abnormal behavior. Maslow even noted in his 1954 classic Motivation and Personality that using immature and ill specimens will only bring about a philosophy and psychology that is of the same caliber – stunted and crippled.

In Maslow's theory, human needs can be classified under five different categories. Another important part of his theory is that there is a hierarchy of such needs or a hierarchy of these different classes of needs. He says that man needs to fulfill the most basic needs first and move up and fulfill the next higher class of needs in the hierarchy until you fulfill everything one level at a time progressing from the basest going up to the most complex.

Maslow's five types of needs arranging them from the most basic (the ones that, according to Maslow, should be fulfilled first) are the following: physiological needs, safety needs, love/belonging needs, esteem needs, self-actualization.

Notice that Maslow lists respect of others, achievement, respect by others, self-esteem, and confidence as needs that belong to esteem (the second highest class of human needs). Now, there are experts in the same field who have challenged and are critical of Maslow's theory.

However, recent research, such as the one published in the Journal of Personality and Social Psychology 2011, show that such needs do exist. However, they do not lend support to how Maslow arranged his hierarchy. It would appear also in some research that it is also possible to fulfill some of the higher needs in spite of the fact that the lower needs described by Maslow's hierarchy remain unfulfilled.

Well, whether you agree or disagree with what Abraham Maslow suggested is another matter. What really matters is that there is evidence that we human beings have a need to be accepted and obtain the respect of others. The fact of the matter is that at the heart of everyone's presentation anxiety is that fear of attaining unfavorable judgment from others. We basically long to be accepted and intrinsically fear rejection.

We can sidestep, cope with, and try to avoid such frightening encounters that trigger one of our most basic anxieties but that will usually just lead to greater consequences. We cannot deny such a need and we cannot deny such a fear. Denial will only make matters worse but acceptance and the willingness to work on the issue will definitely ensure life-long success.

In the end, we end up choosing either of the two paths. At a later part of this book we'll look into these two choices a little deeper. But before moving on, let's look into the diagnosing of what sort of anxiety or fear we are actually experiencing when tasked with addressing a crowd.

Chapter 2: Try Getting Rid Of Fillers

It's best if you wouldn't use fillers while talking. They just make you look nervous, and would make the audience feel like they're listening to a person who doesn't know what he's talking about.

Fillers are any of the following:

Uhm, ah, hmm, ah, etc. (Filler Sounds)
Literally, really, actually (Filler Words)
You know, I think, I guess (Filler Phrases)

Fillers are signs of verbal static—which means that you have gotten suddenly nervous and you have no idea how to go forth with your speech anymore. They weaken your credibility.

So, practice! Here's something you could do to stop yourself from using those fillers.

Make an Assessment

For this, it would be best to seek the help of an audience member—or a friend. Try to make a speech (practice the speech you're planning to use for a presentation), and then ask your friend to keep track of the fillers you have used and their impact on the speech itself.

Make use of a digital recorder so you could playback your voice and hear what you have been saying. Or, you could also record yourself on video—so you could also check your gestures and facial expressions.

Then, answer the following questions:

How much do you use fillers?

Do those fillers distract you and the audience?

Is your credibility tainted?

Slow Down—and Embrace the Pause

One of the easiest ways to combat fillers is to make sure that you slow down a bit. No one's running after you, anyway. No one's coming towards you, and besides, not everyone would be able to understand you if you keep blabbing about without slowing down.

You don't have to be extremely slow, of course, but it would be nice to speak slowly so you could also enunciate the words clearly, instead of making people feel like they don't even know what you're talking about.

Now, when you're about to use fillers, choose to pause instead. Just make sure you won't let it go over 5 seconds or so. This way, you can also create momentum, and you can just ask the audience a question or make a joke. That's definitely better than using fillers.

Be Prepared

Sometimes, you use fillers just because you are not prepared enough. In short, it would be best to:

Relax. Again, try to do some breathing exercises and you'd be able to continue with your speech better.

Learn how to use variations of words. Try to brush up on your vocabulary a bit, and learn at least 5 to 10 variations of words (i.e., very = extremely, incredibly, awfully, exceptionally, etc.) so you'll have a lot of things to say, and you'll be able to express yourself better.

Monitor Your Progress

The next time you make a speech, record yourself again, and check the following:

What is the frequency of filler words in your speech now?

What is the correlation between preparedness and being filler-free?

Have you managed to slow down your pace?

Do you think the negative impact of fillers has already been reduced?

Are you pausing, or are you still using fillers?

Practice makes perfect. Sooner or later, you'll use fillers less—just make sure you have followed the tips given here.

Chapter 3: The Communication Cycle In Ted Talks

As far as the whole process of TED talks is concerned, it entails a multiple number of actors and mediums to make the process successful. Although the efficiency of the spokesman is highly crucial, but the fulfillment of the whole process involving all the agents and elements, together contribute towards the success of the message, is of imperative apprehension.

The major process can be summarized as below.

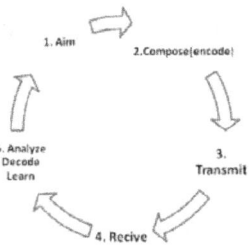

The major participants of the communication cycle

The Encoder-Spokesman

The core purpose of this communication cycle is fulfilled when it is hosted and governed by some potential spokesman. The major function fulfilled by the spokesman is to encode a proper, formalized and compact message. The configuration and indoctrination of this message are highly dependant on the aim of the message. The rationale is outlined so that the encoding can be done in conference with the purpose.

Knowing the agenda, theme or purpose of the message lies at the heart of the encoding process, as it will govern a number of basic decisions pertaining to the whole process of communication. The purpose will govern that which medium will be needed for encoding the message. It includes the vocal or on paper communication. Occasionally the gestures are intended for allocation of meaning to the purpose of communication.

The qualities possessed by the spokesman or mostly appropriately encoder are highly decisive for the effective communication process. The coder must have the extraordinary abilities for making the communication, a complete success.

The decoder- the listener

A message is nothing without a listener or the particular audience, which is intended to be addressed by this process. So as far as the cycle of communication is concerned the listener, the audience or the decoder holds a definite purpose and position.

As mentioned, the encoder will formulate the message depending upon the message content or the aim of the message. However, the message will be coded according to a particular audience and their level of intellect.

The listeners are open for interpreting the message. The message can be highly formalized or it can be a casual message. But in all cases the delivery is objective if it is delivered towards the appropriate audience with related tools and mediums.

But why communication will follow all these steps it is because there is always some purpose, agenda or demand in line with the process of communication. Individual household life the cycle of communication helps the family members to convey little household issues to one another, on the contrary, in the corporate bodies the communication cycle is repeated million times a time with diverse encoders and decoders.

Many experts entail that for highly effective communication the abilities of the encoder of the message deliver are crucial. But the opponents say that the message is of no use unless it is targeted towards the most obvious and potential audience, who possess the necessary skills of decoding and interpreting.

Once the process is accomplished the result is significant in the form of improvement both at the individual and societal levels. A vast portion of learning and improvement is always the result of some substantial form of communication in which the encoder makes use of multiple techniques, and make the decoder aware about the need of the message. Change is always the eventual outcome of effective communication.

Sometimes there are intermediary steps involved in the completion of the communication. The encoder may need some extra efforts for explaining and realizing the importance of the message being conveyed. In this case the encoder may use a variety of tactics and mediums.

Another major intermediary step may invite the critique from the recipient. This critique may result in the continuation or repetition of the process, until the consensus is achieved. The critique is not taken in the negative sense, here it means a form of constructive activity in which both the parties are trying to make the process a mutual and collective success and triumph.

Many people are of the view that the feedback from the listeners or the decoders, serves as the real purpose of success for the communication efficiency. But many of the opponents highlight if feedback is so important than the whole reliance of the success factors is actually shifted towards the audience. So an audience may even underplay the message communicated by highly efficient and smart spokesman.

Chapter 4: How Other Speakers, Past And Present, Can Help You

When we think of people who speak regularly before an audience, we probably think most often of well-known motivational speakers like Zig Ziglar or Dr. Wayne Dyer, but there are many others who speak regularly, many of whom have the goal of urging others to have better lives. These people generally aren't as well-known, but they often give more talks than well-known motivational speakers. Of course, these are priests and other religious leaders, who, like well-known speakers, try to persuade their congregations to lead better lives. And most of these people seem to give their talks with ease. They usually don't seem to be nervous and, in fact, appear not to be bothered much by speaking in front of groups.

For one thing this is probably because they're concentrating so much on what they have to say that they aren't thinking about themselves, but rather about communicating something they believe is worthwhile—something that is important for anyone speaking before an audience. Not only that, but they are intent on the message itself.

There are other professions, as well, that require this sort of commitment to communicating with group. Of course, this includes teachers, lecturers, and professors. In all probability, just like you, many of them were "frightened to death" the first few times they appeared before a classroom or lecture hall filled with students. "What will they think of me?" "Who am I to tell them anything?" "Will they be able to sense how nervous I am?"

This was certainly true of one professor who was just beginning his teaching career. He was totally thrown by the fact that most of the students in his first evening class were a lot older than he was. So he quickly had to decide whether to use the same approach as he had for younger students. Those who continued to teach get past such feelings, and so can you.

A great help, of course, is caring about your subject and wanting to share the information with others. It's forgetting about yourself while you're speaking. What greatly motivates public speakers in that they care. What should greatly motivates you is the same.

Abraham's Gettysburg speech

When Abraham Lincoln gave his now-famous Gettysburg address, the reception was somewhat lukewarm. A London newspaper called it "dull." Now it's considered one of the best, if not the very best, speeches ever given throughout the history of the United States. Noted Orator Edward Everett who spoke at the same event, told Lincoln, "I should be glad, if I could flatter myself that I came as near to the central idea of the occasion, in two hours, as you did in two minutes."

Why is this considered such a great speech and why should that matter to you?

Lincoln's speech certainly didn't waste words. It's terse and to the point. Thus it comes across as powerful. This is because he spent a lot of time in preparation, writing many different drafts. There's a myth that he scribbled the speech on the back of an envelope while riding the train to Gettysburg. But several drafts prove this isn't true.

It can help improve your own speaking skills to read, listen to, and evaluate speeches given by those who are considered among the top public speakers in recent history and in the present. How can this help? You may wonder.

There are two ways. You can evaluate both the presentation and the content. A word of caution, however. Don't try to imitate anyone else. You may note how well the person communicates nonverbally, maybe through eye contact or gestures. This can give you ideas about your own speaking to an audience. But don't try to copy the gestures exactly. What fits one person doesn't necessarily fit another. You need to develop your own style, one that is uniquely yours. You have enough to concentrate on while giving a talk than also trying to do it exactly the way someone else does.

It also can help to pay attention to the content. You can also pay attention how the words the speaker uses and the nonverbal communication tie together to make the speech a unified whole. There are many Internet sites that provide information and examples on well-known and/or well-renowned speakers. Do a search for great speakers—both in the present and throughout history and then listen to the speeches, if possible, or read them to yourself, if not.

Do take into consideration the things you didn't like about them and figure out why. Maybe take notes in two different columns—plusses and minuses. Most likely, however, because these are all excellent speakers, your minus column will certainly contain less than the plus side.

Here are some of the speakers who've made or are making an impact on audiences.

Civil Rights Activist Martin Luther King, Jr. One of his famous presentations is his "I Have a Dream" talk. Listen to it to see why it's considered powerful. Note that he uses a lot of repetition for effect, something that works for him but may not fit the personality or intention of other speakers.

Two others are John F. Kennedy, thirty-fifth President of the U.S., and Winston

Churchill, British prime minister during World War II.

However, the majority of those known today for their skills are motivational speakers.

One of them is Les Brown who most often speaks about people reaching their full potential. Other well-known motivational speakers include Tony Robbins, both an actor and a speaker; Nick Vujicic, born without legs and arms, who urges people never to give up, no matter what. Another is Dani Johnson who inspires people to make money. The list goes on.

Watch videos, available for the most part on the Internet, of as many of these people and others, as well. Compare their styles, their use of verbal and nonverbal communication, and any visual or audio aides they use. How well do you think they do? Why are they so successful? What are some of the things they do that you also might try?

Now apply what you've learned and observed to your next speech. But again, make the speech uniquely your own, using a style that fits your personality.

Chapter 5: Audience

Audience Anchors
Unless speakers and performers are comfortable embracing an audience in, they create walls of separation between themselves and their public. The audience becomes a sea of anonymous, alien faces. This certainly doesn't work, not if an exciting, resultful, transforming event is the goal.

The Egg.

The most important part of speaking and performance is intention, and the simplest, most profound audience-embracing technique I know of, I call "The Egg." Before you get on stage, put you and the audience in an imaginary, giant egg. In other words, in your mind draw an egg-shaped perimeter around the space. "The Egg" counters the rather normal tendency on the part of performers and speakers to keep the audience out, a formula which obliterates the possibility for magic.

One kindred spirit.

If you have serious challenges bringing the audience into your egg, connect with 1 happy, eager, dewey-eyed audience member. Find somebody out there who seems to be with you and anchor in. (You know who I'm talking about here. An audience member with an Alfred E. Neuman grin who bobs his head up and down at each and every salient point.) Speak directly to this godsend. This isn't ideal. Ideal is holding the entire audience in your command and channeling their energy. But it's still better than building a wall.

Avoid looking directly at people who are obviously bored, asleep or flirting with the bimbo sitting next to them. Some speakers have a tendency to lock onto the folks who are not with them, in hopes that they can bring them to the holy land, but this is not a recommended thing to do if you're uncomfortable with an audience.

Three Friends.

If you can connect with 1, maybe you can connect with 3 audience members who are on the same page as you. Split the audience into three sections, middle, left and right and find an agreeable anchor in each section.

As you advance in your abilities to embrace an audience, challenge yourself. Connect with 3 who are bored, not rolling with you, and get them on your bus. Use them as symbols of your ever-developing skills of rapport.

You can mix and match. Pick a couple of audience members who are with you, and a couple who would rather be bowling.

Movie camera.

With a larger audience, once you get comfortable, you can pan the room as if you were filming. Make a sweep with your eyes so you include everyone in your viewing range throughout your presentation. Add a touch of inner recognition — soften your eyes — with the folks who are really on the bus. They're the ones who ride on every word and seem most interested in your remarks. Speaking is a give-and-take proposition. You give out and get back energy and enthusiasm from an audience. Ride the wave.

Jack'S TiDBIT:

It's all about energy. Speakers think they're up there to deliver great material. And of course, they are — but the exchange, the hook, the magic is energy.

Open yourself to take in the energy of the audience.

Ticker Tape

The biggest mistake that speakers can make is to stand in front of their audiences, determined to impart a great impression, deliver dynamic material, not drop a word or miss a beat. In other words, to speak as if a ticker tape is going by. To give a perfect presentation! You can see it in the eyes of speakers when they're in their heads about their material. They look up, to the side, or glaze over. They're not with us, they're at us.

An audience wants to be connected with. Breathe us in, know that we have all the energy that you'll ever need. We have all the words and ideas that you need. Trust this connection. Trust the audience.

Communion.

We Get Our Cue...From You!

The most important thing I can ever say about the speaker-audience connection is "We get our cue...from you!" Your attitude is our attitude. You'll see this sprinkled in numerous places throughout the book. If you're enthusiastic, it's contagious — we tend to be enthusiastic. The more you get into your talk — whatever it is — the more the audience will. If you're having a good time, we tend to mirror you — we have a good time. Conversely, if you're nervous, we start to twitch in our seats. If something goes wrong during your presentation — the microphone doesn't work, you blank out, you find out your zipper is down — the audience looks to you to see how they should react. If you don't make a big deal out of it, neither will they.

Jack'S TiDBIT:

If you ever get lost during a speech — blanked out, frozen — instead of trying to fake it, fess up, ask the audience: "Where was I?"

They're off the hook, and you get back on track.

Audience Tips

√ Know your audience! Learn everything you can about them before you give your presentation.

√ When you've created communion with an audience, each person will feel that you're talking directly to them.

√ Speaking is a symbiotic experience. Let the audience in. Take their energy —

fears, hopes, frustrations, joys — and recycle it back out to them.

√ Audiences thrive on authenticity. They can smell a phony a mile away. That means speak from your heart and not your head. Connect on deeper levels — share all of yourself with your audience. Connect on as many different levels as you can.

√ Remember the holy trio. (Coming up in a few pages) You're not just there to give us content, but to help us feel better about ourselves.

√ To be interesting, be interested. Genuine interest in others is the key to successful speaking — and to productive living.

√ How you view an audience can be the big difference. Audiences want you to succeed. See them as a group of new friends or an extended family — unless you've got one of those families who always rooted for your brother.

√ Give every audience — large or small — your best shot. As Mark Victor Hansen says, "You never know who is sitting in your audience that needed to hear your message on that day."

√ Walk the talk. We're tired of hearing people — who haven't been there — tell us what to do, and how it works. You will be more personally fulfilled and much more effective as a speaker if you really understand the audience's experience — not from reading books or watching movies, but from life.

√ Don't try to control or manipulate the audience. You'd have better luck trying to arm wrestle an elephant. A speaker's job is to give the audience the best that you have, the audience will respond as it responds. Bill Gove says it well, "You are responsible to your audience, not for your audience."

√ Eye contact and a genuine smile go a long way with an audience.

√ There's only one Don Rickles. Never, ever insult your audience, or complain — even if you feel you have a right to (because damn it, they promised you a lectern!). If you encounter rudeness from an audience, raise the level of love and compassion. We get our cue from you; you don't have to get your cue from us.

√ Audience volunteers should be treated with respect, but don't be afraid to have fun with them — but not at their expense. Gift them for daring to volunteer. Give them one of your products. (You do have product, don't you?)

√ Care more about your audience than you do how you look, and you can't miss in this business.

√ Before every presentation — large or small — the most important questions you need to ask are "What action do I want this audience to take, and how can I get them to take it?"

Audience behavior

A last word on audiences. You can't take them personally. Sometimes you look out there, and it seems that if the audience had a thought, it must be to lynch you right after — if not during — your presentation. Remember, we get our cue from you — so you can make a difference by keeping your energy and attitude up. Under any conditions, don't take it personally. Audiences have an unspoken code. Let's review it for a moment. It all falls under the heading "We get our cue...from you." (Am I getting redundant?)

√ Audiences do not initiate, they respond. They expect the speaker to set the tone, the mood and the pace. The speaker tells them how they're supposed to act. (Of course, there are always a couple of ninnies out there, grinning and bobbing their heads even before you get started, and there will be a couple of grumps who would grouse if they had just spent the night with Pamela Anderson.) When you relax, they relax. They will be cool at first, but it's not personal. (Just think about when you're in the audience. I'll bet you're the same way.)

But you're in charge here. Set the tone the way you want it to be. Just because they're staring blankly doesn't mean that this is what they want in return. They want you to be in charge.

√ Audiences want to be anonymous. Audience members, except for those ninnies — don't want to be noticed. Speakers are concerned about their performance. To an obviously lesser degree, so are audience members. Let the audience know — by manner and attitude — that you're not going to embarrass them, and they'll warm up.

Chapter 6: The Audience Is Almost Always Your Friend

It's an extremely common occurrence for someone to be nervous or terrified about public speaking. I'm not going to talk about how I have some magic potion or formula that will make you sound super confident, or somehow make your fear disappear. To me, that is an extremely lofty goal that many books promise, and you know what? I am positive that the overwhelming majority of people who take those kinds of advice do not attain any sort of satisfying results. There's just no way to prevent your sweat glands from producing sweat, or your body from twitching during a speech except with practice and experience.

What I will talk about, however, is what goes on in the mind (or at least probably goes on) of a person who is a natural when it comes to public speaking so that you can understand how it is, in fact, possible to reduce your nervousness. By encouraging you to adopt parts of their mindset, perhaps you can understand how to deal with stage fright. Let's begin with the first positive train that a natural public speaker may have that differentiates himself or herself from an average speaker.

The biggest difference between a natural speaker and the average speaker, in my opinion, is probably the fact that the natural speaker is excited to speak in front of a crowd. The bigger the crowd, the better. They see the audience as their friend, whereas most people see an enemy. A natural speaker focuses on how the audience is going to applause, laugh, or respond in a positive way. An average speaker focuses on how an audience might boo or hiss at them. Think of it this way – most people are afraid of fire. They think about how fire can burn or kill things, but on the other hand, some people love fire. They love how it can explode and demolish buildings so that space for new buildings can be made, and they love how fire cooks food so that we can eat food safely. Maybe this isn't the best example to illustrate this, but do you see what I mean?

For the most part, it may not be a bad thing at all to be fearful and scared to death about public speaking. It just means that you're normal and sane! Most talented public speakers are known to be a little different, and highly eccentric. Need proof?

Think of every massively successful comedian over the last 30 years. People like George Carlin and Chris Rock should come to mind. Do these people seem "normal" or "sane" to you? No, because they have uniquely interesting personalities.

The lesson that I want you to get from this is that as soon as you get excited about public speaking, you will see a marked improvement in how you engage an audience with your words, which will improve your confidence. The bad part about this is that this may be a difficult thing for you to change.

If you aren't able to view public speaking as an opportunity to get excited about, then I would suggest finding the one part of your personality that you not only love, but would also consider to differentiate yourself from others. Find a part that is unique.

You see, your performance is just a natural extension of your personality. If you decide to show an average part of your personality, your performance will be average. If you decide to show something great about yourself, then chances are, that you will have a great performance.

If that's not enough to help you out, then pay careful attention to this next tip. Ready to hear it?

People will almost always sympathize with an unconfident or unskilled speaker, unless than speaker is spouting nonsense. Most of the time, if the audience is not very intrigued by your speech, the worst they will do is just think that you are boring and will probably just think about the speech ending so they can go home earlier.

An audience rarely has the reason to laugh at you in their heads, or make fun of you. If anything, they're willing to be on your side because they are just glad that they aren't the ones up there in front of everyone speaking. You are like their Jesus Christ. The worst that will happen if you are a mediocre performer is that their mind wanders off onto something else.

In conclusion, I'd recommend searching within yourself for that part of your personality that you would feel most comfortable with presenting in front of lots of people at once. Find that part, and magnify it by as much as possible.

Using myself as an example, I'd say that I have natural way of being funny in front of an audience. The way I leverage this humor into a greater effect it to tap into the part of my personality that I love most – which is being a contrarian. When I saw that I'm a contrarian, I mean that I love to do the opposite of what everyone else is doing. For example, if everyone loves red cupcakes, then I'm going to like green cupcakes. If a month later, green cupcakes become the most popular kind of cupcakes in America, then I'm going to love red cupcakes. Do you see the pattern here?

I am merely exerting a part of myself that I regard as integral to my being. By taking advantage of this, I am able to take a stance on the information or issues that I discuss in my speech that helps me to be psychologically strong. By the way, public speaking is a mental game that is about 99% mental, and 1% physical.

That's another thing to remember: if you are able to take a strong stance and explain why you are taking that stance, you have already won much of the battle in giving a great public speech because you are psychologically prepared. It will reflect in your physical gestures and body language. Take my advice and try out this tip the next time you get to speak.

Chapter 7: Treatments For Fear Of Public Speaking

The treatments of glossophobia can be categorized into three: Therapy, Medications and Self-help.

Therapy

A cognitive-behavioral therapy is a common treatment suggested for those who want to be rid of their fear of public speaking. Through cognitive-behavioral therapy, they will learn how to replace the messages of fear that they receive with more positive thoughts and self-talk. This is especially effective for those who experience having panic attacks when faced with the prospect of speaking before a large audience. Through this treatment option, they will learn effective relaxation techniques that they can use to handle these attacks. Once they do get a handle on these panic attacks, they will be easier to control.

According to Page Anderson, who teaches Psychology at the Georgia State University, virtual reality therapy is also effective, especially if the root of the problem is social anxiety. Basically, this type of therapy involves creating a virtual environment where the patients will simulate speaking in public. They will have to deliver speeches again and again, as if they are experiencing the real thing, until such time that they get the hang of it.

Other complementary therapies include hypnosis and psychotherapy. Talk therapy (counseling) and support groups are also highly recommended since the root of the fear is tackled and then talked about with other people who are going through exactly the same thing.

Medications

Medical experts also prescribe certain medicines that would help a person control their nerves or their fear. However, more often than not, these medications are meant to be taken while the patient is undergoing cognitive-behavioral therapy, and not taken on their own.

There are some beta blockers that help one find relief from extreme nerves or terror. Beta-blocking drugs are known to help ease performance anxiety because it has properties that can easily block the action of adrenaline.

Users must be wary, though, of certain side effects that they could suffer when using medications. This is the reason why this treatment is approached with extreme caution. After all, it is more effective in treating the symptoms, but not the problem or ailment itself.

Self-Help

This option often comes after the patient already has a handle on his fear. These methods are aimed largely to ensure that the control that they have over their fear of speaking in public is permanent.

In other words, therapy and medications will help them overcome their fear of public speaking, while self-help techniques will aid in their confidently presenting in front of an audience or a crowd.

How To Choose The Best Treatment Option

Not all treatment options work for everyone. Therefore, when choosing which treatment option to follow, consider the following:

• Cause of the fear. Is it because of a stuttering problem? Was there a traumatic event in the past that the person is having trouble getting over? Or is the person simply too shy to even contemplate speaking in front of two or more people?

In order to know what to address first it is important to know what the root cause of your irrational fear of speaking in public is.

- The real nature of the fear. What are you truly afraid of? It is possible that you may mistake fear of performance as a whole with fear of speaking in public. There are people who are comfortable with speaking in front of people but suddenly freeze up when they have to perform something else, or vice versa. Or it could be the other way around. For example, some actors are comfortable speaking lines on stage, but when they are interviewed, they clam up.

Knowing what you are truly afraid of will let you know if you need to undergo a treatment to specifically fix your fear of public speaking.

- Severity of the problem. In other words, this pertains to the intensity of the fear. Maybe it can be solved by having several counseling sessions. On the other hand, there are also cases where both cognitive-behavioral therapy and medications could be required.

Chapter 8: More Tools For Successful Talks

We briefly discussed some elements of this module previously but, we are going to go far more in-depth here so that you can absorb the information within your subconscious mind. One of the elements mentioned previously was to inject humor into the speech. Certainly, having the ability to make people laugh or smile will always bring your speech to life. People love to hear stories told in a humorous way. While this warms up the audience, it also helps you to relax too. It can even offset the perils of technical problems occurring and humor helps to override these problems.

If you are giving a speech to work colleagues, then, clearly there will be certain messages you will be aiming to get across. If you are able, interject some warmth or humor into the speech, this may not be possible depending on the subject but, if you can, you will see people sitting up and paying more attention. This is important. It creates a stronger connection between the audience and you.

Know Your Subject

You must have a good grounding of the subject matter if you are going to speak with confidence. The more you study the content and understand what you are trying to say, the more able you are to impart this knowledge in an efficient and effective manner. Timing is another issue. It may seem obvious but often this catches people out when they come to realize just how much information they

can add to a fiveminute slot. Equally, the opposite can happen where there is not enough content or, the speaker is talking far too fast. This can put unnecessary pressure on them if they start to run out of things to say. So, planning the content is paramount to success.
- Know the subject
- Time it
- Practice it again

Clearly, practicing the speech reduces this problem but if you are nervous on the day of the event that you may find yourself talking slightly quicker than you normally would. This can be detrimental and so, build in natural pauses where you can look around at your audience and calm your nerves. You are likely to be given a specific time slot and it's important to keep to those timings. Having an abundance of knowledge about the topic you are speaking about will help.

Tip
Slow down and breathe deeply in a controlled way when delivering the speech.

Your ability to relax in front of an audience will depend a lot on the subject matter but also, the type of audience you have in front of you. Note that people will often very quickly spot someone who either does not know what they are talking about or, who does not have much confidence in the spotlight. So, make sure you practice and read up on your topic.

Reading and Connecting with the Audience

A well-seasoned public speaker would always be able 'to read' their audience. If they see the audience beginning to fidget or start to talk amongst themselves, they know they must work to regain their attention. Having the confidence to do this does take time and practice but it is essential if you are going to be performing regularly at public speaking events. Often an audience can be brought back to focus by simply using humor or, through a slight change of topic. This is not so easy to do if you're following a script but over time, you get used to being able to adlib slightly and inject a different point of view or a joke here and there into a well -rehearsed speech.

Always talk to your audience as if you know them. This increases the connection between you. People naturally respond in a warm way to a friendly manner and it is built into us to be slightly more hostile to those we feel are talking down to us. You will always gain more respect from your audience by being friendly and warm but ensure you have a strong sense of confidence running through your speech as well.

Nervousness

Many well-known public speakers are nervous before they get on the stage, this really is not uncommon. Musicians and actors all suffer with stage fright but, being nervous does not equate to being unconfident. You will find that once you start talking, your nerves will slowly abate and once again, having a good knowledge base on your topic will help immensely as your confidence will start to shine through. When you believe in the subject matter, you can talk with ease and this will always build a connection to the audience. It also helps you with any lingering nerves.

Becoming a good confident public speaker takes practice but do not worry if you are always slightly nervous before an event. This is often a good thing as it means you care about your presentation and want to do well. You can learn to use your nerves to your advantage.

In the next module, we will be focusing on this subject in more depth. Make notes about these elements as they will help you to feel more confident and help with the flow of speech:

- Humor
- Research
- Knowing the audience
- Practice
- Understanding nervousness

You will always improve your delivery over time, but you are not there to be perfect. You are there to be the spokesperson with a mission to get your message across.

Chapter 9: Vital Equipment For The Public Speaker

The three most vital tools for the public speaker are Vision, Vocabulary, and Voice.

1. Vision:

Every Public Speaker needs a vision. Vision here refers to the concept of the ultimate achievement towards which we move in life. It is the dream of what you could ultimately be in life.

Every public speaker needs such a vision to motivate him. He/she needs a definite ultimate goal to move towards – something to strive for, something to achieve, something for which it is worth sacrificing; a goal which will bring the best out of him/her.

Most speakers encounter a lot of discouragement as they are daily confronted with temporary failures on stage. They need something, which will counterbalance this and eventually make everything worthwhile, and this something is the Vision. Unless you have an inner awareness of God's ultimate purpose for you, you could be overcome with discouragement and fail to achieve your divinely appointed goal.

2. Vocabulary:

A speaker's vocabulary is composed of the number of words he knows and with which he/she is familiar. Obviously, words are the tools, which a public speaker employs in the pursuit of his profession. The more words he knows and understands, the more fluent and expressive he can be.

Words are to the speaker what paint and brush are to the artist. A speaker can paint vivid pictures with words. As he describes a scene, his audience can almost see what he describes. Words are as important to an effective speaker as tools are to a tradesman.

As a speaker, you must be interested in words by trying to read widely, because reading good literature will enrich your vocabulary. Whenever you encounter a new word you are not familiar with, investigate it by finding out what it means, how it is used in context and then add it to your collection through use.

3. Voice:

Without any shadow of doubt, the voice is the speaker's greatest natural asset. Therefore you should endeavour to take good care of it. You should always be aware of your voice and seek to improve your use of it.

Using Vocalics

Think of your words as clay, and your vocalics (also known as vocal techniques) as the fingers that mould these words into a work of art. Through vocalics, you can create emphasis and achieve a conversational tone that will help win over your audience.

A good delivery conveys emotion and brings words to life, but also feels natural, believable, and not forced. Consider applying these techniques to your presentations and public speaking:

Voice Volume: Shouts as well as silence are equally effective at getting attention. To figure out how loudly you should be talking, first choose the right default volume - the one you'll use most of the time in the presentation. In a small space, the walls tend to amplify sound and make a normal speaking voice loud, so that you would have to quiet yourself down a bit. On the other hand, you'll do better in a large space if you speak loud enough to reach the back of the room - unless, of cause, you're using a microphone.

Speaking in a quiet voice is one thing, but not speaking altogether can be just as effective. A bout of silence lets your words sink in.

Voice Pitch: Raising and lowering your voice can achieve some startling effects. You can add gravity by deepening your voice or humour by lightening it, and even alternate between voice pitches to play the parts of different people in a mock conversation.

Voice Speed: How fast you speak also creates certain moods. Talking quickly conveys excitement and energy, but can easily grate and annoy if you do it too long. Likewise, talking slowly can help complex ideas or very important points go down more smoothly, but after a while it can equally bore an audience. So learn to create a healthy balance for optimum result. Listening to storytellers can give you a good idea how to change your vocal style for maximum effect. Take a look at any book or poetry readings at your local library, bookstore, or coffee shop.

Chapter 10: Sometimes You Will Stink

After only a short time teaching teenagers I discovered some basic differences between years 10, 11 and 12. Year 10 students think they are grown up and most discussions seem to be about sex or innuendo.

Hoping to get "it", nearly getting "it", how to get "it", others who got "some" or might get "some" soon. They also get great joy out of not paying attention to anything an adult says and mocking us wherever possible.

Year 11's conversation broadens a little bit to include when they last had sex and when they are next having sex. Some conversation is about the future but only if it involves sex or parties – and sport or fashion. Adults are tolerated, just, as a means to an end as they are starting to realise that the alternative is paying their own way. Year 12 are no longer showing off as sex is no longer a novelty and they really would like to be away from school and getting on with life. They are kinder to adults as they realise they are not too far off being accepted into the world of self-directed study or paid employment.

Obtaining a short term stint as a substitute teacher, I 'inherited' three different year levels for the final eight weeks of the final term – Year 8 (times 3), Year 10 (times 2), one Year 12 and home room for one Year 8 class. All in all a full teaching load, including 3 days of yard duty - with no supervision. Included in this was a Year 12 Ancient History class.

Above the desk belonging to the now absent permanent teacher (who was on three months' leave in some place un-contactable) was the list of instruction for me to complete the year of study for these students. The note read something similar to this

Grade 8 – Social Studies (pre-history, early humankind)

Grade 10 – History

Grade 12 – Ancient History – The Fall of Rome

I searched the impeccably clean desk for more information:

No class lists

No student assessment records

No 'this is where we are up to' or 'we have covered…..'

Nothing. Zilch. Zip.

Panic!

Every night after class was a long drive home and a mad panic to write lesson plans. Plus I worked for my parents' business from 4pm to 6pm. Not my finest hours. I knew Australian history as it was my major. What did I know about Ancient Rome? Only what I could read the night before class and that they had gladiators, the Colosseum and crazy emperors who fiddled. Russell Crowe had yet to play his part in history lessons.

Prior to this contract I had about 6 weeks teaching experience – total.

The school year in Australia finishes at the end of spring or early summer. The weather is warm to hot and can often be humid.

So, it is not so fond a memory that it was a Year 12 class I was taking on the hot summer day when I had hurriedly left home, dropped my own teenagers off at their school and arrived, harassed and sweaty, at my own school. Catching my breath and settling into the class I realised with horror that I in my haste I had omitted deodorant in the morning routine. Hoping that the class wouldn't notice anything, I knew that back in the staff room I had a spray pack that would remedy the situation.

The class included a moment or two when I had my back to the board. Then out of the corner of my eye I noticed writing had appeared in the corner of the whiteboard. It read "who forgot to put deodorant on this morning?" I still cringe thinking about it. I ignored it of course.

I have since been meticulous about presentation and do a quick check of everything before I get on stage. A long-time friend uses the phrase "wallet, watch, spectacles, testicles" for his leave the house checklist – I haven't created anything quite so eloquent.

As the universe would have it, my life as a high school teacher was short lived. A blessing for all really.

Lesson 4

Have a checklist of things which need to be in place before you speak, which could include:

☐ Remember deodorant
☐ Not too much perfume/aftershave
☐ Check your fly is done up (women too)
☐ Clean your teeth
☐ Lipstick on your teeth? (maybe that's just for women but who knows)
☐ Shoes clean?
☐ Buttons firmly sewn on (reduce the likelihood of wardrobe malfunctions)

☐ Ladders in stockings? (carry a spare pair)
☐ Wear flats until just before
☐ Matching socks/shoes (don't ask, I'm still in therapy)

They may seem standard things to do but when you are nervous about a presentation or the school run causes you to be late, or traffic and the fight with the spouse upsets your routine, or your mother phones on the way out - a mental or written checklist of the basics doesn't go astray.

Have I allayed your fear of public speaking yet? Hang in there it will get better.

Chapter 11: The People And The Place.

Once again we are putting a priority on knowing your audience and about the place where the speech will be given ahead of actually preparing your presentation for a good reason. You will prepare a much different kind of public speaking "product" for your audience depending on a lot of factors about that audience. For starters, how you approach organizing your materials for the speech that you will give can change a great deal depending on whether you know the people you are speaking to or not.

If you are a member of the group or organization and you are essentially speaking to your own, you already understand the values of that group and there is a level of acceptance when you stand up to talk to them. This can be a good thing but it can be a negative as well. An audience that you are quite familiar with may feel more open to interrupt you during your presentation. In many ways, that kind of crowd can be more intimidating than a roomful of strangers.

The make up of the group you are addressing can have a huge impact on how your presentation will be received. By knowing that make up well in advance, you can adjust your choice of language, your arguments or even your topic to fit the background of the people you are addressing.

The age of the audience you are talking to is a big factor for how you prepare your speech. Your talk will look and sound much different if you are addressing children or teenagers than it would if you were addressing a room full of parents. How much are the people you are going to talk to like you? Find the common things you share with them because those areas of shared experience can give you a great deal to work with as you write your speech.

The education level of your crowd is important to how you speak to them. The nature of the group is important as well. You will address a gathering of business people much different than you would a church Sunday School class. Find out if the audience will be all adults or a mixture of adults and younger people or children. Addressing a room full of families means you have to be interesting to the adults and yet be aware of the children because of their ability to create distractions from what you are trying to achieve.

The values of your audience make a big difference too. Even if your goal is to instruct or amuse, values matter. This is especially true if you are seeking to inspire or persuade the people you are talking to.

A persuasive speech always begins with the creation of a need. That need is based on a shared value such as the desire to protect the family from harm or the shared goal to do all you can to make your city a better place to live. If your speech has political or religious elements, the more you understand about how that group thinks together about such value based topics will make a big difference in your success.

It also helps to step back and analyze the psychology of an audience. You don't have to be a PHD in psychology to do that. You can understand how the people you are about to address view you in a very easy way. Simply pay attention to your own attitude toward a public speaker you are about to hear.

There is one important fact about the psychology of an audience that goes back to the myths that make public speaking so difficult. The fact is that almost without exception the audience is inclined to like you and they want to see you do well. Think about how you feel when a speaker comes out. You want that speaker to succeed and you are open to his or her ideas even before that speaker says a word.

Use that knowledge as you prepare your mind and energies to speak to a group of people. Use it to defeat that impression you get as you step up to the podium that the people staring back at you dislike you or are out to get you. That is your insecurities at work. The truth is that they start out on your side. You just have to keep them that way.

Finally, the size of the group you are addressing with have a big impact on how you put together your talk. It will also impact how severe your stage fright might be the day of the talk. We will go into much more depth about stage fright later in this book. But find out from the organizers of the event if you will be speaking to a small group of 5-10 people, to a larger assembly of 100 people or to a mob of hundreds.

While what you have to say should not be affected by the size of the group, how you say it will. If you have to speak into a microphone to be heard, that changes the dynamic of your speaking style. Find out if you will have to use a microphone and if that microphone will be wireless, on a stand or one you have to hold throughout your talk.

By knowing all of those facts, you can practice with those issues in mind. You can also think about speaking to a group where you can see everyone's expression or if that group will be one that is so large, you cannot see everyone who is seeing and hearing you.

These various questions about who you are speaking to, what you will be speaking about, where the speech with be given and why what you will say matters may seem premature to ask before you even write your speech but the opposite is true. The more you know about every detail you will face the day you give your speech will accomplish two important goals. First it will help you visualize the situation you will be in when you give your presentation. That visualization can go a long way to help deal with stage fright.

Secondly, knowing everything you can about your crowd and your environment helps you be more precise in your preparations not only of the content of your talk but in the tools you will you will use to give yours speech. The environment where you will be speaking include the room you will be in, whether you will be speaking form a stage and other factors. Here is a good checklist of questions to ask about your speaking environment.

☐ Will I be standing and looking at a crowd or sitting down?

☐Will the audience be seated in rows or in a circle or semicircle around me?

☐Will I be the only one speaking or will it be a roundtable or panel setting?

☐ Is the room where I will be speaking small enough that I can easily see every person in the audience?

☐ Will I have a podium for notes or be speaking facing a crowd with nothing between me and them?

☐ Will I be elevated by a stage?

Finally, along with the nature of the crowd you are addressing and the particular characteristics of the room or hall, how long is your presentation expected to be? This is a crucial detail because too little time and you will not be able to hit your goals for the speech you are giving. If you have too much time, you lose the audience along with your own sanity trying to figure out how to fill long minutes in front of a crowd. Those minutes can seem like hours.

Once again, use your own experience as a person who has listened to many speeches to sort out how to handle the answers to this question. The average length of a good public speaking address is 15-20 minutes. Think of the average sermon in church. If the speaker keeps his or her thoughts inside of that time frame, you feel satisfied without feeling like finding a way to escape. Once you know how long you will be speaking, tailor the size and scope of your talk. Generally you can make 2-3 good points in a 20 minutes speech if it is not interactive.

Chapter 12: Body Language

The Speaker's Silent Messenger

We need to begin by defining Body Language. Wikipedia records refers to various forms of nonverbal communication, wherein a person may reveal clues as to some unspoken intention or feeling through their physical behaviour. These behaviours include (but are not limited to) facial expressions, gesture, body posture, eye movement, touch and the use of space.

Your body language transmits signals to your audience that are read as part of your presentation. If you are transmitting nervous gestures or are too casual, the audience gets the message. This will strongly affect your message and the way the audience will interpret what you say.

It is important to remember that the audience in a public address is on your side. They want you to be successful in delivering words in a way that adds something special to their day.

Body language can be a useful tool in your public speaking 'armour' if used appropriately. It can add emphasis, excitement and emotion to what you say and help motivate your audience.

Public speaking clubs place great emphasis on teaching their members how best to use their body language to assist their speaking.

As a member of such a club, I learnt the 'Do's and Don'ts' of body language. Here they are listed below.

The Do's Of Body Language

The aims of these 'Do's' are to relax you and to keep the concentration of your audience on what you are saying and not on your mannerisms.

Practise these to gain that attention.

Find a comfortable stance that is not too casual. It must allow you to gesture with ease.

Keep constant eye contact with your audience by moving your eyes around the room so that every person feels you are speaking to them personally.

Smile often. That's easy because it only takes 12 muscles to smile but 72 to frown. So why frown at all?

Lean forward towards a person while listening to their question.

Nod, when appropriate.

Use gesture to add meaning to what you say.

Make sure you maintain close contact with the audience, i.e. stay close to the main body of the room.

Show your enthusiasm for what you are doing in your voice, your gesture and the way you stand.

The Don'ts of Body Language

Here are some of the 'Don'ts' of body language that you should avoid because they can and will distract your audience and lessen dramatically the message of what you have to say.

Don't shuffle, sway, or pace up and down.

Don't be immobile. Otherwise you will lose the visual impact that your body language can add to your words.

Avoid meaningless and repetitive gestures.

No gesture. (This means that your aural communication will not be reinforced because of the lack of visual communication usually given by gesture).

Deadpan expression. By having such an expression you are not using a valuable asset (facial expressions) to convey sincerity and/or the importance to what you say.

Nervous appearance. This gives the impression that you are not sure of what you have to say. So act confidently. You can break the topic up into small manageable slices to ease your nervousness.

Colourless language. This does not add interest or excitement to what you say. It won't excite you either. So your body language will be colourless as well. No one says that when you speak formally you must use boring language. Use words that add colour and excitement to what you say. Make it a goal to look for ways to add colourful language to your speeches.

Chapter 14: Listening And Storytelling

Mindy O'Neall

Topic: Team Building, Impromptu Speaking, Listening and Storytelling

Learning Objectives: This learning activity is designed to promote:

Listening

Retention

Impromptu speaking

Storytelling

Description of Activity: A quick activity that builds skills in articulation and listening while roleplaying in pairs.

Materials needed:

Even number of participants (instructor may need to participate)

Index cards

Classroom

Prep time for students:

Students must complete the assigned readings prior to class

Assignment time: 25-35 minutes

Instructions for Instructor: The instructor should attempt to run the exercise for 35 minutes. The mental exhaustion of the students may be noticeable, and the exercises may seem long. If you notice your class finishing their topics before their allotted time, reduce each time for faster rounds. Be sure you have enough topics as they will run through them faster!

Assign students into pairs. One will be the speaker. One will be listener. These roles will be flipped for each new round.

Give one student in each pair a stack of topics, and instruct them not to look at them.

Instructor reads aloud the details of the activity after pairs have formed and settled down.

The student without the cards is allowed to draw first, and begin the first round.

The student reads the topic and begins to articulate a stream of consciousness. This could be an opinion they have, what they know or do not know about the subject.

The goal for the speaking student is to talk for three minutes about their reaction to the topic.

The goal for the listening student is to remember what the speaker said, and summarize the main points in a one minute debrief.

Instructions for Students: Get into pairs. Move your desks so that you are facing your partner. DO NOT LOOK at the cards I am placing on your desk! Once the students have settled, continue to explain the activity.

This is a timed activity designed to improve your speaking and listening. The person without the cards will speak first on the topic randomly selected from the stack of cards. You may choose any card you like - it does not have to the be top card.

Speaking Partner: You will have three minutes (when I start the timer) to "present" to your partner about this topic. You can tell them your opinion, what you know about the subject, what you find interesting or curious. Stay on topic and construct coherent sentences.

Listening Partner: Listen to remember what your partner is telling you. Notice emotional and physical reactions along with nonverbal used by your partner. Also take note of your listening. Are you formulating counterarguments? Are you questioning the logic used by your partner to build an argument? When the timer rings, summarize for one minute what your partner told you.

Debrief Round: Ask your partner if the summary provided accurately reflects their argument? Reflect with each other and strategize how to improve listening and communication (eye contact, for example, etc.).

After one round, switch partners so the original speaking partner begins listening for one minute, and the listening partner draws a new topic to speak to for three minutes.

Necessary Background: Try open-ended topics where students have some creative authority.

Recent scandals in the entertainment industry

Methods of Survival

Current news

Keep in mind some students are more connected than others, so they to pick major topics of general interest to ensure discussion.

Classic Topics to Consider:

Ice cream or pudding?

Should guns be allowed on campus?

Your favorite vehicle.

Life on Mars

Walmart or Target?

Debrief: Lead a class discussion and reflect on the following:

What did you find challenging about the activity?

What challenges did you face as the listener? Speaker?

What factors contributed to your listening success or failure? What can we learn from this to promote more effective listening?

What strategies did you use to stay engaged?

How did they feel after the 4th topic? After the 8th? Did it get easier or harder? Why?

Topics are the same for every group. Consider comparing the arguments used and their overall level of effectiveness.

Variations:

You can speed up the time, so students have 2 minutes to speak and :30 to summarize.

Add music in the background. Be considerate of other classrooms around you! It is fun to change the theme of the music, and ask students if the different genres changed their tone when speaking/listening.

Use a portable speaker and move around the room so the volume and intensity of the music changes. This adds some chaos, which can make students uncomfortable, but not for long.

Trouble spots: Topics can be duds. Encourage students to continue talking even if they believe they have nothing to say about it. The speech does not have to be perfect! Just keep talking!

Common questions students ask:

Can I draw any card? Answer: Yes.

What if I run out of things to say? Answer: Try your best. Just keep talking.

Chapter 15: Why Be A Good Public Speaker?

Is it really necessary to face the fears and deal with it? Do you need to overcome it? Or can you just ignore it?

Yes! Yes! Yes! There are loads of reasons why you should make that extra effort and fight your demons. And if you fight right, you will definitely conquer them and emerge successful.

Now read on to understand the advantages of a confident public speaker and try to relate how many will benefit you:

Confidence: Empowerment is the key word here. That is exactly how you will feel once you start speaking in public more often. The self confidence will replace the earlier doubts and anxiety. You will be surprised at your new self. And eventually the confidence will help you set a new image of yourself among your peers and colleagues.

Leadership: Earlier you might have kept to yourself and let other do the speaking in a discussion. This would have made you fade into the background. It will not change. While you do most of the speaking, you will be able to put forward your thoughts and ideas. It will also enable you to take leads and guide a discussion. Therefore, your peers will begin to look to you for leadership.

Better Listener: Effective communication will also lead you to become a good listener in order to understand your audience and decide their understanding abilities. You will also improve your reading and writing skill in the process of research and preparation of each public presentation you do.

Performing skills: Yes, non verbal communication is as important as the verbal part of your communication to be able to make the whole communication process effective. This includes the hand gestures, body movements and even voice intonations. Therefore, in the process of preparing for a presentation, you will be developing your performing skills which will not only enhance the information you are trying to relay but also make your presentation more interesting.

More Definite: Vague and apathetic will be out of your attitude towards what actually interests you. If confidence was what kept you from pursuing what actually interests, it will now be different. You will state your point and convince the next person of its validity.

Career Bloom: Yes, a confident speaker in this competitive world will make much more progress and advancement than your shy counterpart. Your confidence and determination will be evident in your speeches and it will attract the attention of your boss for all the right reasons.

Look up to: Can you imagine, earlier you used to be the person sitting possibly at the end of the room or at some corner whereas now, you strive not only to be heard but also make your point in the right way. The younger generation will look up to you for learning. And you might just become their role model.

Networking: In the busy business world, networking has also been a key component for progress. Your way of speaking will assist you to building new relationships and connect with important people. This will in turn expose you to new opportunities which otherwise you would have been shielded from.

Impromptu: Gracefully presenting your case in a moment's notice is a very impressive skill and once you master it, you will win a lot of approvals. Your heart will not beat loudly and your hands will not shake, and your mind will be focused on what you pan on speaking. Nothing can be better than that when you are on stage and innumerable pairs of eyes and ears are on you.

Personal Transformation: While earlier you would be fine with whatever you were able to achieve, this progress in confidence and public speaking will surprise you. You will realize just how much potential you have and eventually you will train yourself to harness this potential.

Source of Motivation: You will begin to derive pleasure in sharing and inspiring others. It will gradually lead people to you for advice and motivation. You will discover the happiness derived from assisting others and the satisfaction that people will seek you out in times of need.

Art of Speaking: Yes, you are right! Speaking is an art. The shear fact that your speech forced people to think beyond their limiting mindsets or it influenced the audience who had a closed mind in the beginning will be a great achievement for you. Your speeches will gradually break barriers in the mind of the audience and they will begin to accept your point if you are able to convince them. A great effect you might have on the masses listening to you!

That is definitely a very long list of reasons why you really need to overcome your fears and walk ahead in life. Think really hard about it as you read ahead in this book.

Chapter 16: The Layout Of This Book –

Answering Your Questions

I decided to do this book a little differently than most. Instead of telling you what I want to tell you, I'd rather address your questions. So I researched the internet to find out the most burning questions you have about giving speeches, and I'm answering them. I know, exciting right? So let's shoot straight to what you want to know most, and then I'll tell you what you should also be asking.

How Do I Deal With Stage Fright?

The biggest question you have is how to get over stage fright. And it's a valid fear shared by most people who are called to speak. And learning to conquer fear and build confidence is one of the keys to impacting in a powerful way from the stage. That's why I devoted an entire book to the subject - book one of this series. So if you are really struggling with this issue, I encourage you to go get book one: The Gutsy Girls Pocket Guide To Public Speaking: Conquering Fear and Building Confidence. It's a quick read.

In the meantime, here are some pointers on dealing with stage fright.

Be prepared. Know your stuff. Practice, practice, practice.

Speak often. Take opportunities to speak where you don't feel a lot of pressure. The more you speak, the more confident you will become.

Use notes if you need to. Don't make it harder than it needs to be. If memorizing the speech means you stand a bigger risk of messing up, then don't memorize it. But practice it enough that you know where it's going, and you can read it without really reading it.

Breathe. When I get nervous I tend to hold my breath. Practice the art of deep breathing – especially before and during the   speech.

Do not picture them naked. (Unless they're hot and then of course picture them naked.) Picture them as friends sitting at your kitchen table. Be YOU, not a polished version of you. Just talk to them like you normally talk, without the rambling and the "ums". Develop a positive inner script. Don't tell yourself that you're gonna bomb. Tell yourself how great you are going to be. Tell yourself how important your message is. If you don't believe in yourself, neither will they. Fake it until you make it.
But don't believe in yourself too much. The only thing an audience hates more than a sweaty speaker who's about to have nervous breakdown, is the diva who thinks she's too good for the crowd. Be confident, but be humble. It's a nice combination.

Why Is Public Speaking Important? Why Do Presentation Skills Matter? When you stand on that stage you exhibit power and an assumed sense of credibility. You are elevated. You have been chosen to command their attention. This is a big responsibility. And people don't like their time wasted. Being an effective speaker/presenter/communicator/connector is a vital asset in life and in business. It's about the art of influencing people. And aside from your actions, words are your greatest tool of influence. If you want to sell, lead, manage, impact, get the job, convince them to pick you, witness, be a powerful politician, write awesome website text, serve customers, get business, raise money, win the pageant crown, get raging fans on social media, captivate an audience, teach, get people to do what you want them to do, or even get your kids to listen to you – then your words and your presentation skills matter. More than you think. And these skills don't come naturally. They must be learned and practiced and perfected.

The art of being an amazing speaker isn't something one is born with. It's a skill that must be cultivated, practiced, and perfected. Just like any other art.

What Is More Important Content or Delivery?

Content is what you say; delivery is how you say it. The two go together. Neither can survive without the other. But there are a lot of speakers out there trying to do just that. You can't have a speech without both. So they are both equally important. An incredible message with no powerful delivery is useless. It's just information. It's just a content dump. It has no emotional impact or influence. An incredible delivery with no message is just entertainment. And while entertainment serves a purpose, it can't be the sole purpose of a speech. The key is to blend content and entertainment. "But I'm not an entertainer," you might be saying. While that may be true, you must still entertain an audience if you want to get their attention and keep it. And with attention spans being so short, your job just got harder.

You don't have to be a good entertainer to impact an audience. But you must entertain them, or they will never hear what you have to say. Attention spans are short. You can't afford to be boring.

Is Speaking An Art or a Skill?

I look at my speaking as an art – a gift that involves a little talent and an extreme amount of work. Like many artists, my art consumes me. I am called to create. I don't do this because I can; I do this because I have to. I can't imagine not doing it. To me, it's like dancing or singing or painting. I create my masterpiece the way I see it in my head, and am fortunate enough to get paid for sharing it.

The more I work at the art, the more skilled I become. The more I study and learn and practice, the more this becomes a skill. I can apply what I learn to my art to make it better.

I think a better question is whether a good speaker is born or created? When I began my career, I had a raw talent that people noticed, and that immediately set me apart. But it didn't get me booked. And it didn't get me standing ovations. The more work I put into it, the better I became, the more impact I had, and the more jobs I got.

It doesn't really matter what you call it. What matters is how you see it. See it in a way that makes you want to work to get better. The rest is irrelevant. Too many people argue over the semantics instead of simply learning to speak better.

I hear a lot of speakers say, "Oh the speaking is easy. It's the selling that's hard." Which is true. But I see a lot of mediocre speakers who are completely forgettable – the chorus line speakers – blending in and offering nothing original. They think their problem is that they don't know how to get the business. When the truth is that their problem is a crappy product. They are trying to sell their way out of the chorus line, and that won't work. The only way to ensure success is to be remarkable on stage. Period.

Chapter 17: Techniques

I use this every single time and it works like a charm. It works like a charm. The first technique is the one that is tried tested and it works even if you look at it from a scientific perspective and that is to take time. The moment you show up on stage once you are on stage take your time. I take 10 full seconds every single time I show up on stage to make my speeches. I know 10 seconds seems like a lifetime. When you're standing in front of a large audience whether it is 10 people or 10000 people. Seconds could mean a lot. It could mean like it could seem like a lifetime. But then if you gather the courage to take the time to compose yourself you'll see the benefits very very clearly see that time gives you an opportunity to compose yourself to gather yourself to cool yourself down to calm your nerves because nobody says that you have to speak immediately on showing up on the stage.

Nobody says that. So there is no compulsion to speak immediately. This is the mistake that most people do. They show up on stage and they think they have to start speaking immediately as though somebody was pushing them from behind. I'm telling you take your time take your time. One of the things that I do the moment they show up on stage especially if I'm nervous is I do barely breathing. I do several takes some very deep breaths with my belly belly breathing is the best form of breathing and it helps calm down the nerves. I get three four five as many as required to calm down my nerves even before I can say my very first word.

Now if you in addition to barely breathing if you're not very comfortable standing right in front of the audience one of the things that you can do is to start shuffling some papers or arranging writing some notes or pretending to do something other than just standing there staring staring at the people. I don't personally do that but then suddenly it is a technique because rather than staring at people you can always do things that will absolve you in shuffling papers buying the time to calm your nerves down. Instead what I do personally is I start scanning the room very slowly as I'm barely breathing. I look at the room from the left to the right very slowly and from right to the left as they absorb the scene as they absorb the people as they absorb the faces trying to look for familiar faces people that I met when they initially greeted them and that gives me the time to compose myself. Tried it works no one other technique that they use which also works is to take the focus of me from me to take the focus away from my own self again like the earlier technique. This works like a charm every single time but it does take conscious practice and that technique is to remember that this is not about you this is not an exercise to glorify who you are.

It's not about adding glory to your personal self.

It is about them.

It's about the audience.

So your entire attention has now to be focused on the audience you are there to impart your wisdom to tell them what you have learned the material that you have gathered so focus on helping them understand what you claim them to tell them.

You are there to teach.

They are there to learn and that is exactly what you are going to do rather than having to think about you yourself your problems your issues with nervousness.

Stop thinking of speech as a conversation.

Pick one person from the audience both and write in the first row or the middle row somewhere a familiar face start right there speak to one person at a time speak to one person and once you are comfortable with that one person move on to the other person so on and so forth.

So the first technique is to take your time.

Don't be compelled to speak immediately take 10 full seconds if that is what it takes. Don't be compelled to speak immediately on showing up on stage and the second technique is to take the focus away from you. Instead focus on the audience start talking to them because you can teach them. They are here to learn, Think of her speech as a conversation. Start speaking to the one familiar person and then move on to the next person so on and so.

So here is a technique that we have seen before but the technique is so important and works so very well that I would like to revisit this in a little bit more detail than before and that is to have a conversation with the group with the audience.

Now before we get to that conversation with the audience let's talk about a one on one conversation that you are capable of having. Would you have any trouble at all talking to one person in the audience.

I hope not.

I'm certain you can have a wonderfully good conversation with one person in the group. If you break it down what is a one on one conversation until you are talking to a person you are fully present in the moment in the situation you are friendly you are animated you are gesturing throwing your hands up explaining things you're having one good time you're free you are dynamic you're looking at how that person is speaking their facial expressions you are responding reciprocating. So a one on one conversation is like magic. We have a conversation without having to worry about how we're doing.

We are in the moment.

The question is What if we can't take all the same characteristics and bring it to a group setting. That same very same things that you do with a one on one conversation. If we can have in a group. So the key here is to be able to learn to hold and one on one conversation in a group setting. Learn to hold a one on one conversation in a group setting. And here is how you do that. Identify one person in the group that you can focus on. Now there is always this one person either you know that person or by virtue of having greeted that person in the beginning you have established a rapport or a connection with this one person but if neither of them happens you don't know the person not to do greet anybody. There is always somebody in the crowd who is eager to listen to your speech and this person usually will be leaning forward will be smiling will be nominated will be acknowledging your speeches nodding his or her head so focus on that person talk to that person.

Imagine that your entire speech is going to be addressed to this one person in the audience and start the conversation. Start the speech like you are speaking to that one person. So as you learn to engage in a dialogue with that one person your speech starts to flow. You are no longer worried about whether he will do a good job. You learn all about it about by that there are a hundred people or a thousand people who are now holding a one on one conversation with that one person. Now once you learn to do that once you're comfortable with that conversation with that one person.

Move on, move on to the next person and then move on to the next person and then move on to the next person so on and so forth. So the key is to be able to learn to hold a one on one conversation with one person at a time and then replicated into a group setting the same things that you would do friendly animated jovial gesturing not having to be conscious not having to be worrying about if you will do a good job. So having a conversation that is the key to a good speech and to conquer any fear in public speak.

Head Nods also called audience of people once you start speaking if you if you believe you still are not sure about what you're speaking are you are still jittery still anxious.

Then one way to get over it is to get the audience to approve what you are speaking about and that is definitely the best way ever to calm your anxiety and to continue to do a great job. So a sure sign of audience approval will give you the confidence to continue to plough through your speeches.

Now how do you get audience approval. You can with one of two ways. One you're already speaking very well we're speaking confidently doing your thing being in the zone. Belting stuff out then the audience will approve your speech. They will smile. They will not and they will engage they will answer questions. So that is what I call the voluntary had nods. People are willing to really involving engaging video with your speech but then there might be situations when you might want to Mileti might want to ask for a head nod. You might want to ask for approval of what you are speaking then which case you have to stop prompting people as you can say things like Hey is that clear. Am I making myself clear? Are you going to ask for a body part?

You can say how many of you have been in a similar situation before. Can I show it. Can I see a show of hands you can ask any number of body questions to continue to validate whether what you're speaking is reaching your audience. So through the voluntary head nods and stimulating head nods you can continue to get audience approval which will give you the confidence that you are doing a great job as part of your speech. Now as you're looking from face to face going from person to person to person there might be situations there might be somebody who either doesn't get what you're speaking or has the frown on the face that says they probably do not approve of what you're saying or they may not understand what you are saying at that point in time. So it's necessary that you slow down and at that point in time and start offering clarifications rephrase what you're saying Give examples that relate to them connect with them and customize your statements so that you can turn that frown into an approval.

You can say things like. Let me explain it a little differently Or what I mean is one other way to say are things like you can say Let me give you a few examples to demonstrate my point. So by clarifying and rephrasing and by giving examples you can help that person understand what you're saying and turn the frown into an approval and had none.

Now the more approval you can get the better the engagement.

So your whole point is to get your message across to the audience.

And one sure way to know that is how much they are engaging with your speech and that you do that through head not whether it is Woland to be constantly.

Chapter 18: Affirmations

Affirmations are positive self-scripts and declarations you can use in moulding your subconscious mind into its most positive form. In recent years, more and more mental health practitioners have utilised affirmations as a component of their alternative practice because they believe that positive affirmations can help in healing their patients who have been hurt by their own negative self-talk and by the negative things they hear from other people.

Promising Results of Research Studies

In 2010, three expert populations (individuals suffering from depression and/or anxiety/panic, esteemed psychotherapists and psychologists and popular self-help authors) were examined under a research study conducted at Arizona State University. The results of the study showed that positive affirmations is effective as complement to traditional treatments in treating anxiety/panic and depression. For certain patients, they claimed that positive affirmations were the most dominant part of their journey towards recovery. All the participants agreed that their own belief and willingness to adopt positive affirmations increase the chances that the affirmations to have real positive effects in their lives. At the end of the research study, it was concluded that treatments for depression and anxiety/panic should be regarded as highly customisable and individualised. As such, mental health experts should create customised treatment programs for their different patients and they should deliberate whether positive affirmations should be included as part of the treatment program or not.

Powerful Affirmations for Treatment of panic.

Here are several positive affirmations you can repeat several times every day so you can start believing in yourself and seeing positive results:
1. I am a confident person.
2. I believe in myself completely in front of crowds.
3. I have full control over my thoughts and my entire life.
4. I am strong and not afraid of talking in public.
5. I am positive and peaceful because I allow my mood to create the physiological response that I desire in my own body.
6. I only let calm and relaxing feelings and thoughts into my mind before a talk in public.
7. My challenges, failures and mistakes open up better opportunities for me to realise my dreams.
8. I believe that I deserve and can achieve all the best things life. I am happy wherever I am now.

9. My feelings are important. As such, I focus on positive things that bring positive vibes in my life.

10. I am comfortable and connected with all people, in all environments.

11. I discover and enjoy the simple pleasures that life has to offer to me at the present moment.

How You Can Practice Affirmations

Before you proceed, you need to recognise that affirmations will only be effective if you have the dedication and commitment to practice them consistently. You may have struggles at the start but you will see that it becomes easier as you spend more time doing it.

You also need to recognise that all the words that come out of your mouth are already affirmations. The sad truth is that most of the time, the affirmations that we utter towards ourselves, about other people and our current situation are negative. But the good news is that you can consciously transform your affirmations and start speaking in a manner that makes you feel more positive and hopeful.

It is important for you to make affirmations as a regular part of your day-to-day life to obtain the optimal benefits and to help alleviate the symptoms of your panic at a faster rate. But you need to always keep in mind that you need to be gentle with yourself. If you are having struggles, take a rest and then encourage yourself to try it again. Remember, this will become easier as you continue your practice.

1. Ponder on your positive traits and qualities. Instead of focusing on what you want to change in yourself, focus on your strengths and positive qualities. You can start with the phrase "I am..."

2. Write down the negative thoughts that you constantly have and wish to change. What do you normally think of when you are feeling worried or scared? Do you always assume the worst? Do

you always tell yourself that you are probably going to panic in these situations? Consider the things you have written in step one and use them to replace the negative thoughts that bombard your mind.

3. Think about positive goals you wish to achieve. What are the specific goals that you truly wish to accomplish? Whether you believe you can achieve them or not, just write them down. As your self-esteem improves, you will find more inspired to pursue your goals. No one is judging you so just write all your goals down.

4. Prioritise your goals and positive affirmations. In the first three steps, allow yourself to write everything that comes to mind. Do not filter out things that you think are petty and irrelevant. It is good to unload all those thoughts in your journal. In step four, your objective is to prioritise which of those goals and positive affirmations you want to tackle

first. Select the goal that you think is the most urgent. Always start with smaller goals. When you accomplish those small goals, you will feel more inspired to continue with the bigger goals.

5. Make it a habit to re-read and re-write your affirmations and goals on a daily basis. Make them the first thing you think about in the morning and the last thing in your thoughts before you go to sleep.

6. Meditate on your affirmations. Spend a couple of minutes every day in a reflective state. You can sit down or lie down but make sure that your eyes are closed. As you do this, think about the goals you want to achieve and your positive affirmations. Allow yourself to feel the emotions that those goals and affirmations invoke.

7. Remind yourself of your affirmations. You can jot down your affirmations on Post-its, scrap papers or notecards and put them in various places

around the house, in your work area and even in your car. Make sure that you always see them as you go through your day-to-day tasks.

Keep at it. Just like other worthy endeavours, you need to continuously practice in order to perfect affirmations.

When you start to see the positive effects of your daily affirmations, be grateful for them and commit to continue with your affirmations. When you do so, you will start to observe bigger transformations in your mood, in your thoughts and emotions and in your life, in general.

Chapter 19: Familiarize Yourself

What makes public speaking such a big deal for so many people is the fact that it combines many different causes of stress and anxiety, some of which go unnoticed. While speaking in front of a crowd and trying to please and impress can create significant levels of stress and anxiety, they are not the only culprits at hand. Another significant source of anxiety is how unfamiliar everything seems. The chances are you won't be familiar with the place you are giving your presentation, creating a certain discomfort as a result. Furthermore, you may not be familiar with the people you are speaking to, making the situation all the more intimidating. This chapter will reveal four ways in which you can familiarize yourself before a presentation that will help to eliminate stress and anxiety, thus enabling you to be at your very best.

Arrive Early

Arriving early can make all the difference when it comes to feeling good about giving a speech or presentation. For starters, if you are feeling rushed your anxiety levels will increase, making the situation worse even before it has begun. This is particularly true in the event that you run the risk of being late. However, by arriving early you eliminate these scenarios, thereby eliminating the stresses they cause. Additionally, by arriving early you can maintain a slower, calmer demeanor, one that will help to regulate your speaking, breathing other functions in a way that significantly reduces the anxiety of the situation.

Another way that arriving early can help is that it can give you a sense of being in charge. When you are the first one in a room, the room becomes yours.

Everyone who arrives after you comes into a room already occupied, thus they are coming into your territory. This can have a huge impact on how you feel about the event overall. By being first, you can feel as though you own the situation more so than if you arrive after the crowd is already present. Anything that increases your sense of being in charge also increases your overall sense of confidence, therefore it is something worth doing.

Become Familiar with the Environment

Being in a strange place can have different effects on different people. Some people will feel excited in a good way, seeing a strange environment as something new and interesting. Others, however, will see the unfamiliar environment as unsettling, feeling nervous and anxious as a result. This can be particularly true in the event that you are already anxious in the first place, such as in the case of giving a public presentation. Therefore, it is always a good practice to become familiar with your environment before the time of your event.

In addition to calming your nerves, becoming familiar with your environment can have other significant effects as well. By walking the room you are speaking in you can get a sense of how the crowd will see you, thereby knowing how you will come across as you are giving your presentation. This will remove any unfounded fears regarding how you might appear or sound, which will increase your overall confidence. Furthermore, you can discover any issues regarding stairs, hidden obstacles or any other feature that might give you problems during your presentation. By being aware of your surroundings you will avoid any mishaps that could serve to derail your presentation, or even worse, cause you discomfort or physical harm.

Become Familiar with the Audience

If you arrive early enough to your event location you will be able to not only beat the crowd, you will actually be able to meet the crowd. This can give you a huge boost of confidence by becoming familiar with the audience you are going to be speaking to. More often than not an unfamiliar group can be more intimidating than a group of people you already know. This is why it can be easier to speak in front of friends rather than strangers. However, in the event that you are speaking to strangers it can make all the difference just greeting them as they arrive so that you can get a feel for who they are.

Another way that greeting people can help is that it can change your perception of the audience altogether. Most people hate public speaking because they feel intimidated by large crowds. If you are able to greet people as they arrive you will begin to see your audience not as a single crowd, but as a group of individuals. This can help to overcome that feeling of being outnumbered. By greeting people as they arrive you will have individual faces in mind as you give your presentation, thus enabling you to feel as though you are talking to people instead of a large, foreboding crowd.

Familiarize Yourself with the Experience
The final method for familiarizing yourself is to familiarize yourself with the experience of public speaking itself. This can go a long way to helping you to decide what methods work for you and what methods don't. After all, there is no single form of public speaking that everyone adheres to. Instead, different people approach the challenge in different ways, usually ones that reflect their personality. By discovering techniques that appeal to your character you will be able to create your own style

of public speaking, one that is comfortable because it feels familiar.

In order to familiarize yourself with the experience of public speaking you will need to attend public presentations given by other people. It is important to see more than one presenter so that you can experience different presentation styles and formats. This will give you several choices when it comes to how to give your presentation, including the format of the material, any visuals used and how interactive you are with the audience. You might also witness someone make some of the mistakes you are afraid of making. In this situation you will be able to see how they address and overcome their mistakes, giving you insight in what to do should you experience them yourself. This will remove the fear of the unknown, leaving you with the tools needed to overcome any obstacles you might face.

Chapter 20: Practising Your Speech – Useful Techniques And Equipment.

Nobody really likes to listen to a recording of themselves speak but, if the speech is important, I record my rehearsals and listen to them. These days this is very easy. I can and do use my computer, a digital voice recorder or my smartphone. This allows me to evaluate my delivery.

It is now very easy to make a video recording of your rehearsals. You can use a camcorder on a tripod or have a friend record your rehearsal on a smartphone or tablet. This not only allows you to respond to any faults in your delivery but also allows you to see yourself as others see you. This allows you to identify and respond to any mannerisms. It even allows you to evaluate the suitability of what you are wearing. I am very untidy so I know that I need to check that my tie is correctly knotted, that my hair has been combed. I also have to polish my shoes and tie my shoelaces properly. I have also realised that a freshly laundered suit is essential as a rumpled jacket and baggy trousers do not create a favourable impression!

Some commentators suggest that you look at yourself in the mirror as you rehearse. This suggests that you can practice your expressions. If you do this, however, your expressions and gestures will become artificial.

I occasionally use an application such as "PrompterPro" to help me practice and time my speeches. This particular 'app' has a teleprompter view for scrolling document text. It can also record and play back audio files. The speed of the scrolling can be arranged to coincide with the speed of delivery.

Practise reading aloud

It can be useful to practise reading aloud as if to an audience.

This will help you:
- become less self aware
- verbalise what your eyes are reading
- judge the volume, speed and pitch of voice needed when speaking to an audience
- see that silences and breaks contribute to the quality of delivery
- practise appropriate emotions according to the content of what you are reading
- help you realise that you can lift your eyes and look directly at an audience even if you are reading aloud as you will remember the end of a sentence or verse of poetry

Suggested task: Try reading out a railway timetable — and make it sound interesting!

We must practise until we are familiar with what we are going to say. Practising our speech may well lead to rewriting parts of our original material.

- We can shorten sentences if we find that they are too long. We then rewrite them.
- We can decide where we need to pause, and how long the pauses should be.
- We can decide where we need to raise or lower our voice.

Practice will help us decide how we will deliver the speech.

We can, for example, get rid of words or phrases that are difficult to pronounce.

If these cannot be eliminated then we need to practice and rehearse them until we are happy that we can pronounce them correctly. We might have a foreign sounding name, for example, that we cannot avoid using. In order not to cause offence (or laughter at our efforts) we need to practice the name over and over again.

The more familiar we are with the speech, the less nervous we will be when we deliver it. We are also less likely to be too dependent on notes or a script.

There is, however, one obvious danger. The more often you practice and the more familiar you become with your text, the more likely you are to deliver it at too great a pace. This is not obvious to you because you have the text in front of you and your eyes can read it more quickly than you can say it.

I do not advocate learning your speech off by heart, though I understand that the famous orator Cicero did so. You might forget what you are supposed to say and 'dry up'. In addition, there is a very high probability that you will deliver the speech far too quickly.

I suggest that you have a 'critical friend' to listen to you when you rehearse. A genuine 'critical friend' will tell you tactfully what you need to do to improve. A really 'critical friend' will probably give you the same messages but without considering your feelings. Whatever kind of 'critical friend' you have, it is better to have constructive criticism in private than to make errors in front of a crowd (which is possibly the main reason why most people are frightened of speaking in public.)

In addition, you need to have a copy of the speech to which you can refer both when rehearsing and delivering the speech.

You can mark the script in the light of your private feedback and either keep this marked copy or make a new copy for the actual presentation.

I also have a second spare copy of my speech in my briefcase and possibly a third in my car-just in case!

Chapter 21: It's All About Your Audience

Public speakers exist for the purpose of delivering messages and to share ideas with other people who are willing to listen to them. Without audiences, there would be absolutely no reason for speakers or presenters to do what they do.

Sadly, many presenters, writers, and performers of all types fail to realize that, without audiences, they would not have any reason to present, write, or perform. Do not make this mistake as you prepare your speeches and your presentations for those that have committed time to listen to what you have to say. They are not nearly as interested in you as they are in the information you are going to give them.

Everything you do and everything you say during your speeches and presentations should be done and said to enhance the experience of your audience members. This point cannot be overstated. It does not mean that you cannot tell a personal story or a funny tale during your presentation; it does mean, however, that if you choose to talk about something personal or emotional, your reason for doing so should be to either enhance the connection between you and the audience, or to drive home an important point in relation to your topic.

In order to deliver the best possible speech or presentation to a given audience, you are going to need to do a bit of research and find out as much as you can about the people who will be in attendance the day you present. Let's look at some of the information speakers should have about their audiences prior to Presentation Day:

How much knowledge will the audience have about the topic of discussion? Are they people who have no background regarding the subject of the speech? If their understanding of the topic is limited, then the speaker is going to have to spend at least some time discussing the fundamentals of the subject. For example, a business owner who is going to be addressing a group of high school students about leadership is probably going to talk a lot more about the definition of leadership than he would if he was presenting on the same topic to a group of fellow business owners.

What values are important to the members of the audience? Does the audience share common values or are they more diverse in terms of their belief systems and behavior? Speakers who are able to gather this information regarding their audiences are better prepared to compose a presentation that will be interesting to a greater number of people. If the speaker is scheduled to speak in front of a group of people who are mostly conservative in terms of values, it doesn't mean that he or she can't discuss liberal principles. However, it does mean that the speaker's audience may be a bit more contentious in regards to the material being presented than an audience made up of people who are more liberal-leaning.

Do audience members share similar educational experiences? Having an idea of your audience members' educational backgrounds is important because it will allow you to present your material in a way that will not cause people to "tune out," which they will do if you are speaking over their heads and they do not understand what you are talking about. By the same token, if you have tailored your presentation to an audience that you assumed to be made up of high school-educated folks and you end up presenting to a group that is made up mostly of people who hold master's degrees, then you are most likely going to have some problems with audience attention in that situation as well. Do your best to tailor your presentation so that your audience members can not only understand it, but also benefit from experiencing it. If your audience is diverse in terms of the education demographic, you should make sure your presentation is simple enough for all to understand.

Do audience members share common or diverse demographics such as age, race, residency, socio-economic status, religion, or sexual orientation? Knowing as much as you can about the demographics of your audience will help you as you plan your speech or presentation. Presenters need to be sensitive to diverse groups in order to avoid offending audience members. If you are presenting to a group who adhere to different cultural norms than the norms with which you are familiar, take time to learn about those norms so that you can avoid using language or nonverbal communication that could offend your audience. For example, holding two fingers up in the United Kingdom may be seen as an insult, whereas in the United States it can be interpreted as a positive sign. Audiences will appreciate your efforts to present your information in a way that shows that you care about them and that you are sensitive to their differences.

Audience Expectations

As we have stipulated earlier, there are many different occasions that call for public speakers, and the expectations held by each audience are unique to that occasion. The expectations for a best man who is charged with toasting the bride and groom at a wedding ceremony are vastly different than the expectations for a woman who is asked by her family to eulogize the passing of her favorite aunt. Know what the expectations are, and then work to tailor your speech and your delivery to fit those expectations.

If speakers are well-known by audience members, they will probably not have to introduce themselves and spend too much time discussing their backgrounds. However, if there are audience members who are not aware of the speaker's background and the qualifications she possesses in regards to the task at hand, then she must spend some time letting them know who she is and what qualifies her to speak on the matter before her.

Questions to Ponder:

What information do you think is important to find out about your audience prior to a presentation?

What methods can you use to learn as much as you can about your audiences prior to your presentation?

Chapter 22: Use Of Visual Aids In Your Speech Or Presentation

Adding visual aids to your presentation or speech is very effective. There are basically 5 (five) types of visual aids used. These are:
- Power point slides
- Model
- Video
- Handouts
- Flip chart or chalk board

Power point slides

Power point slides are the most used visual aid technique in speech or presentation. In almost every presentation, the speaker uses power point slides to deliver the speech effectively. However, making slides according to the audience demands is one of the key points to be remembered. For example: power point slides for a group of children will be different than for professional workers. Some of the important points while making the slides are:

☐ Slides should format according to the demands.

☐ Not more than three points in every single slide. Providing more points in a single slide will not allow the audience to look into it properly.

☐ Colour selection should be done according to the theme of the presentation.

Model

☐ It should be large enough so that everyone can see it properly.

☐ It should work accurately according to the requirements. Prepare back up plan in the case of mechanical failure.

☐ Show each & every part properly to the audience.

Video

Third most popular option of visual aids is to use videos related to the presentation. The video should convey the main message of the speech.

Handouts

Handouts are one more option of visual aids. Distribute them to the audience before or after the presentation or speech. Make them as a single sheet of paper with clearly defined all the points, graphs related to your idea.

Flip charts or chalkboard

☐ Write clearly in large letters & if possible with different colour chalks.

☐ Write the highlights instead of writing the whole sentence with maximum number of words per line must not more than 6 (Six) & maximum number of lines per page must not exceed 6 (Six) either.

☐ Avoid using unfamiliar & complex abbreviations.

☐ While writing, you must also maintain the eye contact with the audience. You must not block the chart or the board either.

Tips for question answer session

☐ Have good listening skills. Listen to the questions completely & carefully.

☐ Answer those questions which you know correctly. If you don't know the answer, simply reply them like ' I will get back to you when I will have the answer'. Never use the phrase like 'I don't know the answer'.

☐ Never use the phrases like 'your question is not correct' or 'don't ask more question' etc.

☐ Keep your answer short & avoid making eye contact in the end of your answer with the person who asked you the question. This may allow the person to ask more & more questions.

☐ Keep your points clear & never use any sentences to answer the question which eventually go against your main concept of the presentation.

☐ Use evidence instead of your opinion.

Chapter 23: Bombshell

Amonth passed before I heard any word back from them. Fellow speakers were getting anxious and I'd learned from one that her talk was about to be uploaded to the TEDxBasel website in the coming days. Apparently there had been hold-ups in the editing process.

Then one morning, sitting at my desk in the tallest building in Switzerland, an e-mail arrived from Jane that hit me like a brick.

She began by saying it made her sad that we couldn't find agreement on the matter, and stated that my talk would not be posted at that time. She stressed that it had been a difficult decision and more time would not be invested to revisit it.

She then stated that I was a "poor ambassador" for TEDxBasel and I had not appreciated the effort put in to make my talk a success, adding that it was inappropriate to continue endorsing our relationship.

Bizarrely, Jane finished by saying that I gave a great talk, and she was happy to have given me that chance.

You can no doubt imagine how I felt. Six months' work would now never be seen again. I assumed that sharing my experiences with my friend O'Patrick, who then shared his observations with Jane, constituted being a "poor ambassador". There was nothing else I could think of.

Now, you'll have discovered that I am a man of letters. The reason I appeared on the BBC when I was 14 years old was because I wrote to the television presenter, Alan Titchmarsh, and asked to be on his show. You don't get anything unless you ask.

Incensed by this decision, rather than respond to Jane, I decided to write to the

Head of TEDx at TED headquarters in New York:

Dear Mr Herratti,

I was a speaker at the TEDxBasel event in Switzerland on 28th May and I have today been informed by the organisers, Jane and Harrison, that my talk will not be published. Considering the tremendous amount of work that I put into this talk as a speaker, this is extremely frustrating and I am disappointed that my idea will be spread no further.

The reason I have been given is that I used the word "bullshit", once, in my talk. Considering that my topic was about corporate bullshit, this word was quite unavoidable. After using it once for the necessary impact, I subsequently used alternatives.

I met with the organisers following the event, who told me that they intended to edit out the line. I asked not for an edit, but would agree to a bleep. They have today informed me that as we could not reach agreement, my talk will not be posted.

I find it incredulous and totally against the principles of TED -- the whole reason why I agreed to do the talk -- that people like this, who are trusted with the licence for TED-branded events, should be allowed to impose their personal views and exercise such heavy-handed censorship. I wrote my talk for an intelligent TED audience and not for an audience of schoolchildren. In addition, the organisers have refused to release the feedback results from the audience; I have information to suggest that the highest rated talk of the event was mine.

I would be extremely grateful if you could look into this matter with some urgency.

Yours sincerely,

Peter Sandbach

Five days later I received a brief, unsigned response that simply thanked me for being a speaker, apologised that

I'd been having trouble with the organisers, but finished by saying that the decision to publish my talk rested with them. He did, however, say that he had contacted the organisers and told them that he would accept a bleep over the word "bullshit".

At the same time, I had written to the other speakers at the event to try and conjure up support. Over the next few days I received messages from several fellow speakers, sharing my outrage at this situation. One of them even said she wished all the speakers could be happy to see their talks online, and that mine not being there would be a shadow on the day.

Another speaker told me that while she supported my position, she did not feel comfortable speaking out about it. It was clear to me that this news must have filled them with the fear that their talks could also be pulled in such a fashion if they spoke up against the organisers.

Chapter 24: Don't Walk Like A Tiger On The Stage

After a long time, I visited a zoo that day along with my friend who has some special interest in wildlife and is also studying wildlife. We were standing in front of the cage with a tiger inside and I noticed that the tiger was moving from one side of the cage to another side to and fro and I said, "Wow! What a walk" and my friend looked at me and said, "No Praveen, you should not be happy about this walk.

I asked him the reason and he explained that in wild life it's called Zoochosis stereotyping behaviour by animals in captivity, having the same routine every day they are under stress, they are in panic and because of this stress, nervousness, and panic, they are moving continuously from here to there. This is called pacing and they are not even aware they are doing this. This is happening automatically".

This is sad, but the reason I'm sharing this with you is so many times we have seen people on the stage doing the same thing repeatedly. You must understand one thing if you don't like stage, stage is as good as a cage for you, a virtual cage because you can't come out from that stage or that virtual cage unless you're finished, people are watching

you, so when you are in this virtual cage and when you don't like the stage, you don't enjoy the stage.

You do something similar, you move from one end of the stage to another end continuously. We have seen so many people doing this or they go backward and forward in a cyclic or a rhythmic manner. People move on the stage but when they are doing this, they have not told their legs to move, they are doing it automatically.

But at the same time audience is watching all this and speakers might be giving clues to the audience that they are nervous, that's the reason their legs are not under their control and they're moving automatically. Now a few people say "Praveen come on, you should move on the stage".

Of course, you should move on the stage but only when your legs are under your control.

There has to be a purpose of moving on the stage but this kind of movement, going forward & coming back or moving from one end of the stage to another end of the stage, will add no value to your presentation, or your talk, or your speech, on the other hand, might distract the audience, so what we should do? Two things, first identify whether you have this problem or not. Maybe you don't have it, but I have seen so many people with this problem. And one of the biggest reason they don't overcome this is that they don't identify it.

Firstly, self-awareness is very important. So next time when

you are going on the stage ask your friend, your loved one, or maybe you record your video on your smartphone and check whether you are moving backward forward unknowingly .Whether you have not told your legs to move still they are moving, if answer to this question is "yes I'm moving".

Take conscious efforts of putting your legs straight and stand on both your legs. Don't move. You can give a world best presentation by just standing on the stage but move on the stage only once you have your legs under control. Sometimes in my workshops I keep paper pins on the shoes, so if you're moving they will fall down.

So after the presentation, they have to be there on the shoes or I hold their legs from behind, why? Because after one or two exercises like these, the legs will be under the control of the speaker. But why we should do all this? Because you like it or do not like it, if you want to be a leader in your life, you have to stand on the stage like a leader and speak with your legs under your control.

12. 5-point scale to evaluate the impact of
your presentation

How do you evaluate the impact of your stories Mr Praveen? I remember that day, few speakers were sitting together having a good time and in the middle of the discussion someone asked this serious question to me and I said, "Sir, I have very simple five-point scale to evaluate the impact, let me share this five-point scale, because when you are going on the stage next time whether you share stories, or presentation, or talk, even you can consider using this five- point scale to evaluate the impact of your content on the audience.

For this, you have to make yourself available for the

audience after your talk, maybe in the tea break, lunch break or after the conference, whenever, but you should be available, accessible, visible, approachable, for the

audience.

Now imagine for a moment that I just completed my talk, in a conference. There were around 300-400 people sitting .

after my talk when the conference was over. Now I am available and standing in a corner.

Audience is free what they want to do now but if no one is coming to speak to me after the conference, I will give myself on this scale 0. Why? Because I have not even broken that barrier, they are still not comfortable coming to me and speaking to me.

Modern speaking is when you speak on the stage, audience should feel, "yes he just like us we can speak to him/ her", but if they are not feeling comfortable coming to me and speaking to me, zero on the scale.

But if they are coming to me and they are saying "Thank you very much for coming here sir, and we are so glad that we could host you, we are very happy that you have come, do come again". If they using these kinds of phrases, on this scale I will give 1, not more than that.

If they're coming to me and they say, "Wow! we just loved the way you spoke on the stage, your body language, vocal variety , the way you were moving on the stage, the way you were interacting, the way you made us laugh. It was very interactive" I would give myself 2 on the scale.

But if they're coming to me and they're sharing a similar type of stories that I have just delivered from their life.

Message from their perspective. If someone is coming to me and talking something like this, would give myself 3 out of 5.

Now, what is 4? I remember when I gave my first TedX talk, I spoke about the disease which is very common, more common than diabetes and hypertension. Many people are suffering from this disease and the name of the disease is SWM "Someone Watching Me" disease and in that talk, I had given the message that no one is watching you from outside, that someone is inside. So don't worry about the world, so after this talk, I was just standing there and one person came to me and he said, "sir, can I speak to you"? I said, yeah please go ahead.

He said, "I have attended many conferences, after the conference I always wanted to speak to the speakers, but I'm not doing that great in my life and I used to feel that ,if I speak to them and if someone sees that he's speaking to speakers, someone will feel "come on, he's just wasting the time of the speaker" But this time I decided to speak to all

the speakers because now I know that someone is not outside but that someone was inside me.

So if someone is taking action on the message we have just delivered, it's 4 out of 5 on the scale.

What is 5 ? I remember i gave one talk in one Institute and

the whole talk was about, wherever you are in your life, you are the output of your own decisions. stop blaming others and then one day suddenly after few months actually I was traveling somewhere and I got a message, "Thank you very

much for the talk. I was completely frustrated because of my studies and I was about to tell my dad that I'm not going to study now, it's enough But then after listning to you talk I realized there's something wrong in me. I have to take some efforts," when people change their perspective because of your talk because of your stories. I will give 5" .

When you change your perspective, you take action in your life, because I've heard so many times a lot of speakers coaches, trainers, they claim that they have changed 10,000 lives, 20,000 lives, maybe 1 million lives , but I believe that you can't change so many lives. You can change only one life that is yours. As a Speaker, as a storyteller, we can change the perspective of people.

Fifth is, that you have changed someone's perspective and because of change in perspective that person is taking action in her or his life and because of that action that particular person is changing his or her life, and when something like this happens. It is 5 out of 5.

Chapter 25: Practice Makes Perfect

> "There are always three speeches, for every one you actually gave. The one you practiced, the one you gave, and the one you wish you gave."

As much as I have talked about practicing, you know I just had to make a chapter about it. I know many of my visionaries may say, how do you teach someone to practice?

I'm going to be honest, I had to learn how to practice. I didn't know what I was doing and that was why, for a while, I didn't receive results. There is an effective way to practice and an ineffective way to practice. Just because you are doing something, it doesn't mean you are doing it right. The worst thing to do is do something wrong over and over again, with no results. That is also the definition of insanity.

You should practice more the shorter your talk is

Now I know when I said this earlier a lot of people were confused about why you would practice longer for a short talk than you would for a long one. The reason is because you have less time to make the same impact. You have to be able to give the value so that a person is going to want to give you their value. Their value of course is their contact information or their money, aka coins as I call it.

When you are introducing yourself, doing your "elevator speech," you should practice this every single day. Starting with your introduction, to your body, to your closing. I always tell my students in S.Y.S.T.E.M. Mastery that every time they open their mouths, they should be collecting coins and/or contacts.

Otherwise, what is the point of talking about what you do?

The way that I practice is simple. I draw out my talk with the tables identified and the legs. I then put it up on the wall and time myself for each section. Next, I create PowerPoints based upon my talk. For most of my talks I have a standard introduction. From one that is standard for when I'm at networking events, to one that is standard for when I'm doing a talk that is longer.

I make sure that when I practice I go all the way to questions and answers if I am planning to give time for them. Some may think this sounds crazy, but I will even pretend that people have asked questions and rehearse the answers. I want to always be fully prepared. If you fail to prepare, you will be prepared to fail.

Record yourself and watch yourself

After you have practiced a few times, you'll want to record yourself. You don't have to get any fancy equipment or anything. Simply get a cheap tripod that has a device to hold your cellphone and use your cellphone to record yourself. The reason that you want to record your talk is to be able to see yourself and some of the things you may do that you didn't realize while you were talking.

For example, how many times do you use filler words like "uh", "um", "ok", etc.? How many times do you move from left to right? Are you using your hands or holding on to them for dear life? How about your tonality? Are you changing that up as well? These are things you most definitely want to pay attention to. Remember, your body language is oh so important.

Start with smaller groups then grow

Now another thing I make sure to do is record myself when I'm actually delivering my talk in front of prospects. If I have a big workshop coming up, I will always do a shorter version to see how I do. You can practice all day long, but let's be honest: when it's show time, sometimes you may get nervous and forget it all. The only way to get through being nervous is repetition. During that repetition is the best time to record yourself so you can see how you operate under pressure. This is going to help you tremendously.

Smaller groups will also allow you to be more intimate. I like to always open up for more questions and answers in smaller groups, because it will help me to determine if I need to tweak my talk. I also like to give out blank cards so people can tell me what they think.

Have a speaker's coach watch you

One of the best things I could have ever done was hire a coach to watch my talks. That's not all they did in regards to my talk, but that was a great incentive. All that they taught me on creating a talk that sells I am now able to teach my students.

While you will do your talks in front of others and be able to watch yourself, it is absolutely key to have someone who knows a bit more see your talk. This way, they can point out things that maybe you are doing or not doing that you didn't catch.

Chapter 26: Pitch Perfect

Selling already makes many of us uncomfortable. Combine that with public speaking, and you are really onto something people really hate to do. As speakers, to make our biggest impact, we must sell a solution we have in the form of a product or service.

Therein lies the problem.

We need to start crafting offers rather than selling a product or service. We need to highlight the problems we solve. Our products and services are designed to either take away pain, or create pleasure.

Once you learn to craft an offer, you will separate yourself from other competitors. Most people try and sell a commodity; but that is the worst thing you can sell, because when you are selling a commodity it's a race to the bottom.

If you're a bit confused with what an offer is, let me share this;

We cross paths in town and you mention you are out shopping for a new iPhone. You mention the latest iPhone is retailing for $1000 at all the stores you have been to.

"Why don't you buy my one off me? It's only a week old."

"How much?"

"$2000."

Obviously, you could go to any of the stores you have just been to and buy a brand-new phone for half the price. Why then would you spend twice as much for my phone?

This is where a well-crafted offer comes into play.

"Alright, this is the deal; when you decide to buy my iPhone right now, the first thing you're going to get is an iPhone." The retail price is $1300, and you can get those anywhere, so it's not that special. Remember you are trying to sell a commodity at the moment. We need to turn this into an attractive offer.

"When you buy this iPhone, you get a couple of other things. First, I know you are an influencer looking to improve your public speaking, branding, and positioning. Over the past ten years, I have bought multiple different courses from the world's leading trainers in speaking, branding, positioning, and online marketing. Not only that, I have created my own trainings on Podcasting and Public Speaking. All of these have cost between $1k - $15k dollars. When you get this phone, all of those will be linked on the DropBox app installed there. I would estimate that you would be getting $120,000 worth of training all in the phone ready to go.

"Secondly, you will get direct access to my secret Voxer link. On here, you can ask me questions 24/7 about anything to do with your business, positioning, or speaking career. I will answer you within the day. People pay thousands to have access to this, and when you get the phone it will already be linked.

"Finally, this phone has all my contacts in it; I am talking the worlds leading event organisers, trainers, and C-Level Executives of some of the worlds largest companies. Usually the phone costs $1000 but you get all of this for $2000."

That is an offer. Selling the same thing but making it something of value to the customer. Of course, this wouldn't work if someone wasn't interested in personal development, support, or contacts (Not that I would give any of your contact details away if you are in my phone!), but for those who are interested, it's an absolute no brainer.

Understanding the offer is half the job done. We now must show the value of this offer to your audience.

If you have ever been on a sales webinar or an event with a product offering at the end you would have seen this is play for one reason. It works! Having interviewed hundreds of people who have successfully sold millions of dollars' worth of products and services from webinars and stages, 'the stack' is the one similarity they all share.

Here is the basic framework and psychology behind a killer stack. There are certain pre-requisites for this to work effectively:

You haven't over-taught in your presentation. If you are selling from stage, it is important to show a lot more of the 'Why' rather than the 'How'. This may seem like you are under-delivering, but it isn't. Too often, I see speakers jump straight into the how. You need to take them on a journey to first highlight their problem, and then show them the solution and why your product or service is the right solution. If you jump straight into educating them on the how, they will get to the end of the presentation thinking they have the solution to all their problems. The likelihood is that they don't, and by doing this you are doing them a disservice and having less of an impact.

Do your research! To have an effective pitch you must know your target audience. Understand what their biggest problems are, their pain points and fears, as well as their goals and aspirations. You need to know them better than they know themselves. One big mistake many make here is that they assume they know all those answers. Stop doing this. Have meetings with your target clients and ask them specific questions. Write down the exact answers they give and use them in your presentation and sales copy. If you have your target client identified correctly, then they won't be the only ones experiencing the exact same problem and fears. They will also use very similar wording to express it. Do this well and you will come offstage and the audience will be saying "It felt like you were talking just to me!".

Be confident with it. Most of us are scared to ask for the sale. This is reflected in your close. Be confident in your products or service and know you are doing something that will value your audience.

Creating the stack.

You are going to come up with a series of elements that make up your offer. Each one is designed to overcome an objection that your audience has. If you overcome all their objections, then the only logical thing to do is purchase what you have on offer.

Each industry and setting circumstances will vary but use this as your framework. With each element, you want to put a price on these if they are individually sold or offered.

For illustration purposes, we are going to use a podcast training product I use to market via a webinar.

Element #1: The Opportunity: This is the big training product or service they will receive. For most pitches, this is where people begin and end. If you do this, you will leave a lot of potential customers on the table. For my podcast training, this was a Six Week Masterclass. During the presentation I would go over each week, briefly ensuring that it was clear as to how this would get them to their end goal.

Element #2: The Tools: Describe to your audience what your offer will provide. This can be software hardware, or even templates such as excel and swipe files. These tools are designed to solve an objection for the person to help them achieve their goal. I offered swipe file templates for my podcast students to use for reaching out to new guests, setting up pre and post interview emails, and nurturing campaigns. This allowed them to just edit to suit and get the same type of results with their guests as I did.

Element #3: Tangible #1: During most webinars or sales events, you will go over three points or as I learnt from Russell Brunson's 'secrets'. This leaves intrigue, as people want to know what the secrets are. In your stack you will have a tangible solution to each point/secret you teach. My first secret I reveal is how to find the topic and style of your show, and creating an idea avatar for it. The tangible solution I then offer in my stack is an exclusive private community to get brainstorming and fine tune their ideas before creating.

Element 4-5: Repeat for each point/secret you talk about. At this stage you want to restack all the previous elements you have mentioned on a slide with the individual value and the total value at the bottom. This anchors the value and price into their minds.

You follow this up with what we call an if/all series. This is where you further anchor the price based on the result your offer will create. Each if/all statement relates to a different one of those tangible elements and the current total you have on your slides.

"If all the training did was give you clarity on your podcast style, approach, and launch strategy, would it be worth $xx?"

"If all the templates did was save you four hours each week and connected you to world leading influencers in your field, would it be worth $xx?"

Leave them with two options. Usually, this is gets them carry on as they were and continue getting their usual results or products, or entices people to try and do it themselves, aiming to avoid all the mistakes you did; wasting time and money in the process. The other option is to find a proven system, product, or service to fast track the process or make their lives easier.

Element #6 Exclusive Bonus: Scarcity is brilliant to get people who are on the edge to act. Give a bonus that makes this a no brainer decision. Access is a great option for most products and services. Giving them access to a member of your team or a one to one call with you has very high perceived value. It might also be something like an extra period using the product or service or a free or discounted period.

Present the new addition onto the stacked slide with the new total before explaining how this is how much it would cost to get these individually, but that you are going to package this together for a special price. Briefly go over each point and repeat the individual price to anchor the value then reveal the discounted offer.

Compare and challenge alternatives: Here you can compare and challenge other alternatives such as doing it themselves, or hiring someone else new or within your team to do it. I wouldn't give direct competitors a comparison here.

Guarantee/Risk reversal: For those of your audience who still have objections, a money back guarantee for a period of time takes all the risk out of it for the potential buyer.

Urgency/scarcity bonus: Finally, follow this up with the price and add emphasis to the bonus for those who act now, or the certain amount of people you are offering it to for early action.

You can then finish with questions and answers, if time permits. Take note of the questions you get asked for future presentations, as these are often objections you have not handled throughout your presentation or close.

With each element you go over, it's important to not just present what is on offer, but also highlight what problem it is going to help solve. This can be saving time, money, resources, using a proven system, overcoming fear; and the list goes on and on.

I like to use a case study to highlight a lot of these.

"Take Anna, for example. She is extremely busy running four different companies, and doesn't have time to be worrying about creating new templates and working it all out herself. She was able to pass those templates and workflows to her assistant to set up, and now she doesn't have to do all the heavy lifting. Anna told me these templates save her at least five hours a week, and without them she never would have started on the journey to create a podcast."

As much as people want to trust and listen to you, they can often relate to others who are at a similar or closer stage to them. Also, if you offer a product not in your audience's wheelhouse, like marketing for service-based industries, they won't relate to you; but they will to your client's experiences.

To get your audience to a point where they are okay with a pitch, you must highlight the problems to make them aware of it. Show them the solution and demonstrate you have that solution. Just like any good story or talk, you must take them on a journey and allow them to relate to the road blocks along the way. If you do this, then the simple solution is for them to work with you.

Your challenge is to take whatever you sell and figure out how you can package it into an offer. Break down the solution into those multiple elements and relate them back to the problems your audience is facing.

Do this and the sale will take care of itself.

Conclusion

Once you get the hang of it, you will find that speaking is a really beautiful thing. It is educational, it is entertaining and it brings you closer to people.

But you have to start speaking for all of that to happen.

You now know how you can begin doing that, whether it is for a date or an autograph. Or, speaking on stage in front of a thousand people!

All the best to you!!!

www.ingramcontent.com/pod-product-compliance
Lightning Source LLC
Chambersburg PA
CBHW072012070526
44583CB00015B/1440